SeX PisTOLS

I WANNA BE ME

PALAZZO

First published in 2022 by Palazzo Editions Ltd
15 Church Road
London, SW13 9HE
www.palazzoeditions.com

Text © 2022 Dave Simpson
Design and layout copyright © 2022 Palazzo
Editions Ltd

Every effort has been made to trace and
acknowledge the copyright holders. If any
unintentional omission has occurred, we would be
pleased to add an appropriate acknowledgment in
any future edition of the book.
A CIP catalogue record for this book is available
from the British Library.

Hardback ISBN 9781786751249

Bound and printed in China
10 9 8 7 6 5 4 3 2 1

Designed by Amazing15 for Palazzo Editions

SeX PiSTOls

ANNA
ME

DAVE SIMPSON

40 132

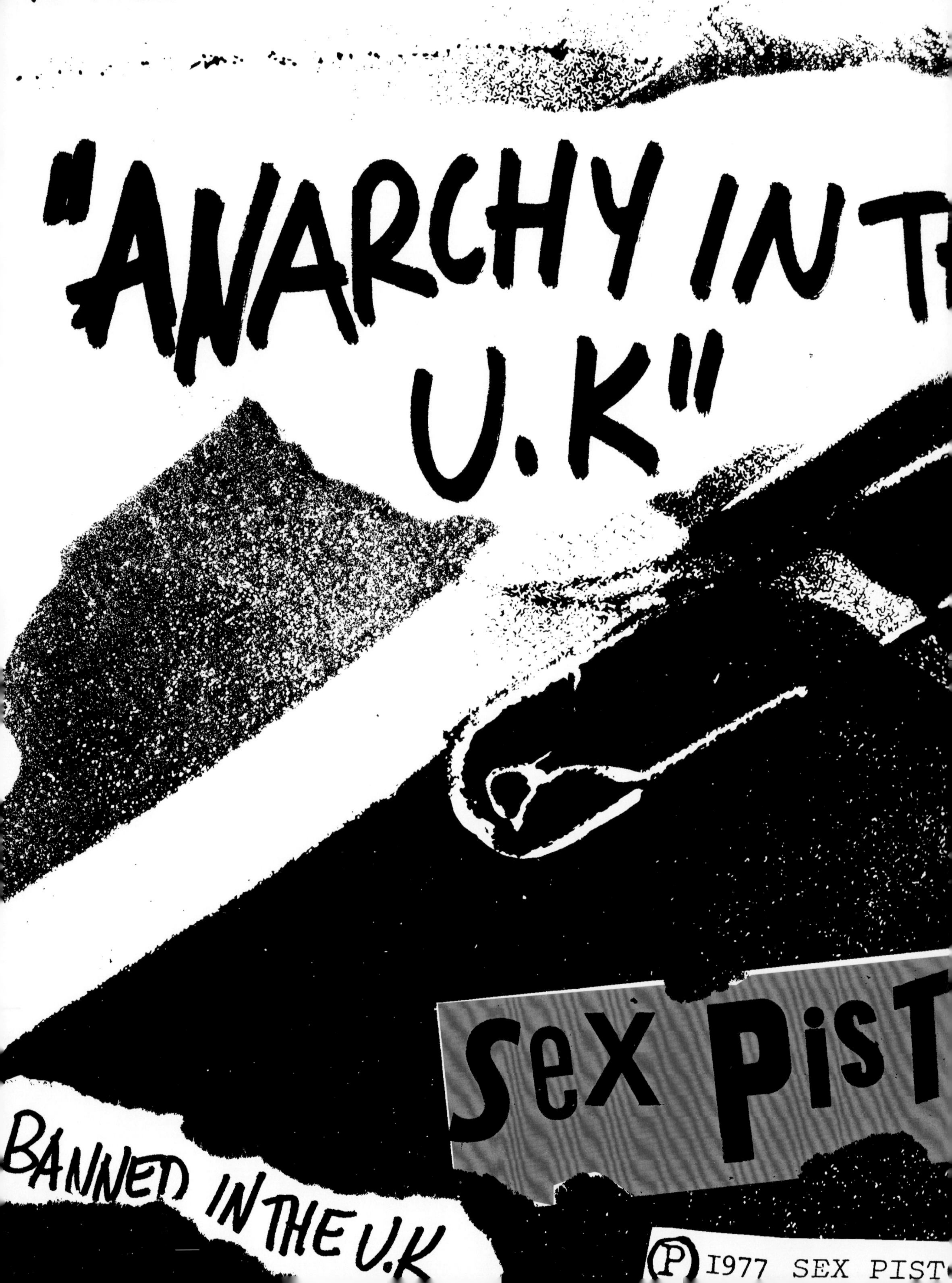

CONTENTS

INTRODUCTION

"Get off your arse!"

Sex Pistols singer Johnny Rotten yelled at viewers of Manchester-based Granada Television show, *So It Goes*, on 28 August 1976, rocketing eyebrows and raising blood pressures in sitting rooms around the north. It's hardly the way a rising "pop group" would begin their broadcasting career today. In 1976, it felt like regional television's equivalent of an alien landing. Groups just didn't behave like this.

The charts from that week encapsulate the pre-punk British music scene. At the top – where it had spent the past six weeks – was Elton John and Kiki Dee's "Don't Go Breaking My Heart" – an up-tempo, cheery number from the British pop superstar and his able vocal foil. A very decent pop record, if hardly the sort of thing which would persuade a generation of teenagers to tear up their old clothing, smash their parents' records and start a new youth movement. At No. 2 nestled another member of pop's aristocracy – Paul McCartney – with "Let Me In", by his post-Beatle supergroup, Wings. Other chart high-fliers ranged from amusing period ditties such as David Dundas's "Jeans On" – to the gentle easy listening of Dr Hook or Lou Rawls. Disco's emergence as an increasingly powerful force was represented by 5000 Volts' "Doctor Kiss Kiss" and Abba's sublime "Dancing Queen". The Swedish band had an unlikely influence on punk rock, of which more later. In 1976, such songs provided the feel-good soundtrack to one of the hottest summers in memory. Notably absent was any kind of *edge*.

As Britain sweltered, the simmering tensions starting to bubble up around the nation were not reflected in the music. Unemployment figures in 1975 were the highest since the Second World War. Inflation had rocketed, while the OPEC oil crisis had pushed the country into recession. The UK was enduring endless crises, such as slashed public expenditure and the three-day working week, brought in as a measure to conserve electricity, because coal stocks were low due to industrial unrest. And the post-war "consensus" of British politics was collapsing as neither major political party seemed to have answers. Mounds of uncollected, rotting rubbish piling up in Leicester Square seemed to sum up a nation in need of emergency surgery.

The Sex Pistols stepped into this void of brewing discontent with Johnny Rotten's challenging words chiming with a generation of youth who were desperate for someone, anyone, to offer something more exciting and reopen pop's old generational gap between teenagers and their parents. The singer's cry of "Get off your arse!" was just the start as guitarist Steve Jones's marauding guitar riff roared in and *So It Goes*, the British music show for Granada TV, provided the unlikely platform for the first broadcast anywhere of "Anarchy in the U.K.", one of the most memorable and influential singles in British pop history.

Opposite – Being an anti-Christ is sooo tiring: Sid Vicious and Johnny Rotten (John Lydon) outside a pub, 1977.

The show's presenter, long-haired Tony Wilson [who was also a pop impresario, nightclub owner and latterly named 'King of the Manchester music scene'] introduced the Pistols, who appeared after the now-forgotten twiddly prog types Gentlemen and equally twiddly folk types the Bold Brothers. The punks' arrival at the end of the programme blew the billing to smithereens. The opening line of "Anarchy in the U.K." set the tone for the next three incendiary minutes and became the sonic bomb that the Pistols placed under not just British pop but the establishment in all its forms, from TV stations to the monarchy. *"I am an anti-Christ, I am an anarchist. Don't know what I want but I know how to get it. I wanna destroy God's supply. 'Cause I want to be … Anarchy,"* yelled Johnny Rotten, in his indignant, furious pomp. Most viewers were probably more appalled than excited, but to a small – and rapidly growing – section of Britain's alienated youth, the Sex Pistols were the exciting answer to their wildest dreams and their parents' and hairdressers' worst nightmares.

Now, decades later, it's easy to forget just how revolutionary the band were. In 1976, they looked very different from anything that had preceded them on the programme or anywhere else. Rotten's spiky hair, safety-pinned torn jacket and general disaffected air provided an early glimpse of the punk look that would soon become instantly identifiable in towns and cities and lead to howls

of "What have you done to your hair?" from those that didn't understand. The band's sound wasn't quite as radical. They were foremost a rock band, distilled from influences such as the Who and the Faces, with a different energy to the rapid-fire riffing of US counterparts-of-sorts the Ramones (who, in another premonition of where pop was headed, Wilson had also mentioned on *So It Goes*). However, nobody before the Sex Pistols had sounded so angry, so appalled, so genuinely thrilling.

"Anarchy in the U.K.", released three months later on 26 November 1976, reached No. 38 but was the beginning of a chart reign which saw seven Top 10 singles and a seminal, hugely influential No. 1 album in 1977's *Never Mind the Bollocks, Here's the Sex Pistols*. The same year, the single "God Save the Queen" – controversially and some say illegitimately kept off the top spot by Rod Stewart – had the dual honour of attacking British deference to the Royal Family in the Queen's Silver Jubilee year and becoming the most heavily banned or censored record in British pop history. The Sex Pistols burned very brightly but briefly. Their entire career lasted just two-and-a-half years from formation in 1975 to a messy, acrimonious split in January 1978 (followed just over a year later by the death of bassist Sid Vicious). However, what they lacked in longevity they more than made up for in cultural significance.

Above – Sex Pistols Johnny Rotten (vocals) and Steve Jones (guitar) perform at the Electric Circus, Manchester, UK, on 18 December 1976, one of the few "Anarchy Tour" dates that wasn't cancelled.

Opposite – The Sex Pistols attempt to look very serious, London, 1 May 1977.

Arguably, no British band since the Beatles has done as much to shape the nation. Musically, the Pistols' impact was enormous and continues to resonate. The group heralded "punk rock" and have inspired generations of bands – and alternative music as a whole – ever since. Their influence stretches from punk and post-punk to Bob Marley (who celebrated a kinship in "Punky Reggae Party") to the Rolling Stones, Guns N' Roses through to the New Wave of British Heavy Metal, dance music, industrial and EDM. The Pistols spent their career on major labels (three of them, inside 18 months) but in inspiring Manchester's Buzzcocks, whose self-released *Spiral Scratch* EP dented the Top 40, they sowed the seeds that led directly to record labels Rough Trade, Factory Records, Mute, today's labyrinthine independent sector and a DIY musical ethos that stretches from limited run singles to home recording.

Meanwhile, the punk look – initially created by manager Malcolm McLaren and designer Vivienne Westwood – has become a staple of high street fashion. Prior to punk, high street fashion involved flares, kipper ties and lapels wide enough to eat your dinner off, but in came tight PVC

Above – Johnny Rotten, manager Malcolm McLaren and friend, outside Marlborough Street Court 11 March 1977. The singer has just been fined for possessing illegal substances.

Right – Punk Rock fashion hits the high street. Models Jordan and Simon wearing Pistols "God Save the Queen" T-shirts from McLaren's shop, *Seditionaries*, King's Road, London, 18 May 1977.

Opposite – "Taxi for a Mr. Vicious?!" Sid Vicious, Johnny Rotten and Steve Jones, London, 10 March 1977.

Pages 12-13 – Sex Pistols frothing at the mouth, 1977.

trousers, sloganeering T-shirts and spiky hair. Meanwhile, Jamie Reid's seminal Pistols artwork (for the record sleeves and associated political artworks) remains a major influence on graphic design and art. Countless novelists, broadcasters, film-makers, poets and even politicians have taken something from them. Christopher Nolan, the director of Batman movie *The Dark Knight*, has said that Rotten inspired his film's depiction of the Joker character's "commitment to anarchy, to chaos" because the Sex Pistols have become a go-to reference for uprising or rebellion.

It's often felt that the Pistols' underlying manifesto is one of nihilism – and certainly the closing words of "Anarchy in the U.K." – "Get pissed, destroy" – suggest that. However, behind such misanthropic statements lies a deeper message of the power of individual thought and action in the face of seemingly unsurmountable barriers. The B-side, "I Wanna Be Me", said it all:

"Now is the time, you got the time, to realise, to have real eyes … Don't wanna be someone, need to be someone. I wanna be me." The band's less celebrated legacy is in showing that four miscreants from ordinary working-class backgrounds could be anything they wanted to be – and in their case shake the foundations of society in the process. In 1976 and to this day, the Sex Pistols showed that there are other ways of doing things and there are alternatives to the norm or the pre-ordained.

What were those instructions again? "Get off your arse!"

THE FILTH aND

THE fURY

Freddie Mercury's toothache altered the entire history of British pop. It certainly changed the fortunes of the Sex Pistols.

On 1 December 1976, the singer's band, Queen – who scored a famous No. 1 with "Bohemian Rhapsody" the year before – were booked to play on Bill Grundy's London ITV teatime show, *Today*. However, Freddie's molars had other ideas. The star normally avoided dentists, but the pain was so bad he needed to make a rare visit, meaning Queen could not appear on *Today*.

The band's label, EMI, had a conundrum: they didn't want to let down or irk the producers of a programme which provided a valuable platform for their acts. So they offered an alternative: their newest signings, the Sex Pistols, could be made available. It had only been weeks since Rotten and Co. had signed to EMI, releasing "Anarchy in the U.K." just three days earlier, and they were in the middle of a campaign to promote it. *Today* agreed. The timing suited everyone. Or so it seemed. What happened next would make the Sex Pistols the most controversial band in the country.

According to bassist Glen Matlock, the band weren't actually that keen on appearing, as it meant them being dragged out of rehearsals. "We very nearly didn't do it," he reminisced in *Classic Rock* magazine, years later. "This big limousine turned up. [Being] punk rockers we were like: 'We're not getting in that thing …' Then this phone call came through from [Sex Pistols manager] Malcolm McLaren saying: 'If you don't do it your wages will be stopped this week.' We were all in the car like a shot."

Left – This bare-chested frontman's emergency dental work changed the course of pop. Queen. L–R: John Deacon, Freddie Mercury and Brian May performing onstage.

> ## "IF YOU DON'T DO IT YOUR WAGES WILL BE STOPPED THIS WEEK. "
>
> ### *McLaren*

The band's entire slot was just 90 seconds. What could possibly go wrong? The Pistols turned up with a small entourage – common amongst huge artists but more unusual for a new group. What's more, the people with them weren't the kind of lackeys – make-up artists, security and the like – that would normally accompany a major group. The band arrived with the soon-to-be-better known "Bromley Contingent", a bunch of suburban London followers (only two of them actually from Bromley) from whose ranks would soon step the punk (then post-punk) band Siouxsie and the Banshees. On *Today*, the Contingent ranks consisted of Susan Ballion aka singer Siouxsie Sioux, Steve Chaos (who would become Banshees bassist Steve Severin) and their friends Simon "Boy" Barker (a keen punk photographer who went on to front Vivienne Westwood's

World's End shop) and "Simone". Vivienne Westwood was and is an iconic fashion designer, and was then Malcolm McLaren's partner.

As was standard for such a programme's guests, the whole group were taken to the "green room", where they could prepare for the show and avail themselves of ITV's generous hospitality, including alcohol. Bizarrely, ITV's archaic telephone system at the time meant that any unanswered calls were diverted to the green room, meaning that, since producer Martin Lucas had left them there alone, the Pistols and entourage were able to greet unsuspecting callers with a shower of abuse. With hindsight, ITV could possibly have pulled the plug on the whole thing then, but this was nothing compared to what would follow.

If the Pistols were a primed hand grenade, presenter Bill Grundy was an unlikely sort to

Above – "It all went off": Pistols and punks on Bill Grundy's *Today* show, ITV, London, 1 December 1976.

pull the pin. The 53-year-old was a veteran broadcaster and presenter who'd started out at Granada, previous work ranging from TV drama to a column in *Punch* magazine (a weekly humour and satire publication) to playing himself – as interviewer – in the film version of popular Seventies sitcom *Man About the House*. Grundy's demeanour when interviewing the Pistols – apparently prompted by having met them before the show – is one of unimpressed belligerence. It is as if he is wondering why on earth someone of his talent and reputation should lower himself to interview these reprobates. Fatefully, the regional news pro-gramme was broadcast live and uncensored in the days when four-letter expletives were not allowed to be broadcast, even after the 9pm "watershed", after which children were less likely to be viewing.

On cue, the show cut to the seated band: Rotten, Jones, Matlock and drummer Paul Cook, with the "Bromley Contingent" standing behind them. Provocatively, Barker had chosen to wear a swastika armband for shock value rather than to demonstrate any fascist leanings. Jones opted for a T-shirt from McLaren's SEX boutique depicting uncovered breasts. Rotten was at his provocatively mischievous best, having been given an unexpected opportunity to publicly reject the school and class system that said working-class boys like him should know their place. "We didn't 'know our place'," he reflected years later in the autobiography *Anger is an Energy*. Hence, at teatime on 1 December 1976, Bill Grundy's show became the vehicle by which the UK witnessed the moment a youth uprising was catapulted to national attention.

"They are punk rockers," began Grundy, nearly thrice the age of his guests, to camera. "The new craze, they tell me. Their heroes? Not the nice, clean Rolling Stones ... you see they are as drunk as I am ... they are clean by comparison. They're a group called the Sex Pistols, and I am surrounded by all of them ..."

"In action!" Jones quipped, reading from the autocue and thus anticipating what came next.

"Just let us see the Sex Pistols in action," continued Grundy. "Come on kids ..."

A two-minute film of the Pistols performing the Stooges' "No Fun" to a jostling bunch of early punks, including Siouxsie, was shown, after which Grundy did his best to appear aghast, banging his sheet of interview questions on his knee.

"I am told that that group have received £40,000 from a record company," he grumbled. "Doesn't that seem, er, to be slightly opposed to their anti-materialistic view of life?"

"No, the more the merrier," Matlock responded.

"Really?"

"Oh yeah."

"Well tell me more then."

"We've fuckin' spent it, ain't we?" sneered Jones, prompting Grundy to ask, "I don't know, have you?"

"Yeah, it's all gone," Matlock continued, cheerily.

"Really?"

"Down the boozer," said Jones.

"Really?" spluttered Grundy. "Good Lord! Now I want to know one thing ..."

"What?" asked Matlock.

"Are you serious or are you just making me, trying to make me laugh?"

"No, it's all gone. Gone," Matlock insisted.

"Really?"

"Yeah."

Grundy explained that he wasn't asking about the money, but about the band's approach in general. "No, but I mean about what you're doing."

"Oh yeah," insisted Matlock.

"You are serious?"

"Mmm."

Grundy tried a new approach. "Beethoven, Mozart, Bach and Brahms have all died ..."

Rotten now entered the fray. "They're all heroes of ours, ain't they?" he said, sarcastically.

"Really ... what?" asked Grundy. "What were you saying, sir?"

"They're wonderful people," Rotten continued, and could hardly have sounded more withering had he practised.

"Are they?" asked Grundy.

"Oh yes! They really turn us on."

"But they're dead!" offered Jones, prompting Grundy to counter, "Well, suppose they turn other people on?"

"That's just their tough shit," muttered Rotten, under his breath, deliberately or more probably unwittingly handing Grundy the opportunity to begin removing the metaphorical hand grenade's pin.

"It's what?"

"Nothing!" insisted Rotten, trying to move on. "A rude word. Next question."

Grundy wouldn't let it lie. "No, no … what was the rude word?"

"Shit," said Rotten, calmly and matter-of-factly.

"Was it really? Good heavens, you frighten me to death."

Not unreasonably, Rotten seemed slightly irritated by this and replied "Oh alright, see if …" before his voice became inaudible. Grundy turned his attention to the Bromley Contingent, particularly – and unwisely – the young women.

"What about you girls behind?"

"He's like yer dad, innee, this geezer?" Matlock snorted.

"Are you, er …" spluttered Grundy.

Matlock continued: "Or your granddad."

By now, Grundy's focus had turned to Sioux, who was visibly preening to satirise the much older male presenter's unwelcome attentions. "Are you worried, or are you just enjoying yourself?" Grundy asked.

"Enjoying myself."

"Are you?"

"Yeah," smiled Sioux.

"Ah, that's what I thought you were doing."

"I always wanted to meet you."

"Did you really?"

"Yeah."

"We'll meet afterwards, shall we?" he asked Sioux, who responded with an exaggerated pout.

Grundy's behaviour had become far too much for Jones. "Dirty sod!" he told the presenter. "You dirty old man!" With the credits about to roll, Grundy detonated the invisible hand grenade.

"Well keep going, chief," he told Jones. "Keep going. Go on, you've got another five seconds. Say something outrageous."

"You dirty bastard!"

"Go on, again."

"You dirty fucker!" Jones responded, to widespread laughter.

"What a clever boy."

"What a fucking rotter."

"Well, that's it for tonight," Grundy concluded. "The other rocker Eamonn [referring to fellow *Today* presenter Eamonn Andrews] – and I'm saying nothing else about him – will be back tomorrow. I'll be seeing you soon. I hope I'm not seeing you again. From me, though, goodnight."

"*YOU DIRTY FUCKER! … WHAT A FUCKING ROTTER.*"
Jones

Right – "Go on, say something outrageous": Rotten and Jones preparing responses on the *Today* programme.

This wasn't the first time anyone had used the F-word on British television. Famously, in 1965, theatre critic Kenneth Tynan responded to a question on the BBC's *That Was the Week That Was* (a satirical and irreverent programme about current events) about whether he would allow sexual intercourse to be depicted on stage. Well, I think so, certainly," Tynan said. "I doubt if there are any rational people to whom the word 'fuck' would 'be particularly diabolical, revolting or totally forbidden. I think that anything which can be printed or said can also be seen." This caused a furore and Tynan even received death threats. Earlier, in 1956, a somewhat refreshed Irish poet Brendan Behan was interviewed on *Panorama* and had appeared to slur the word. Then, in 1959, Ulster teatime programme *Roundabout* had asked a man painting the Stranmillis Embankment railing in Belfast whether the job was ever boring, to be told, "Of course it's fucking boring." Actor Miriam Margoyles claimed to have inadvertently used the expletive when she got a question wrong on *University Challenge* in 1963. A decade later, on teatime news programme *Nationwide*, broadcaster Peregrine Worsthorne had been asked how he thought the public might react to the news that Conservative minister Lord Lambton had been found in bed with a sex worker. "In all probability the public would not give a fuck," he answered. In 1970, an episode of *The Frost Programme* (one of the most popular and influential political TV talk shows at that time) had broadcast an arguably even more offensive swear word, when Felix Dennis, editor of *Oz* magazine (which itself would be subject to an obscenity trial the following year) informed presenter David Frost

that he was the most "unreasonable cunt" he'd heard in his life. However, for the F-word to be aired on peak time regional news as it was on *Today* – hours before the 9pm watershed to an unsuspecting news audience – was still way beyond the pale in 1976. Moreover, it was being used not by a famous theatre critic or celebrated poet, but by young punks calling themselves the Sex Pistols …

The reaction was immediate. The *Today* switchboards lit up and presumably many calls were still being rerouted to the green room. One caller, 47-year-old Kent lorry driver Jason Holmes, claimed to have been so outraged by what was on screen in front of his eight-year-old son that he kicked in the screen of his brand new £380 TV set.

The following morning, the tabloids weighed in. "The Filth and the Fury!" screamed the front page of the *Daily Mirror*, unwittingly providing director Julien Temple with a title for his acclaimed 2000 Pistols documentary. Underneath the *Mirror* headline, the article referred to "uproar as viewers jam phones" and "panic when the air turned blue" with "the filthiest language ever heard on television." Ray Mawby, Conservative MP for Totnes, lodged a formal complaint with the Independent Broadcasting Authority, who subsequently said they had "accepted assurances from Thames that the incident, in which foul language was used by the group, was regrettable but unavoidable."

In 2015, Matlock rather downplayed the incident when I spoke to him for *The Guardian*. "Steve had downed a bottle of Blue Nun and it all went off. We were young." At the time, though, the consequences were swift and far-reaching for everyone concerned.

" UPROAR AS VIEWERS JAM PHONES … THE AIR TURNED BLUE [WITH] THE FILTHIEST LANGUAGE EVER HEARD ON TELEVISION. **Daily Mirror** "

Daily Mirror

Grundy in rock outrage

BRITAIN'S BIGGEST DAILY SALE

Thursday, December 2, 1976   No. 22,658

dge in urder' ardon ocker

NOT McWHINNIE

D G E made an nning attack yester- the way a man ed of murder was royal pardon.

old a jury: "You ell have come to ar conclusion that s rightly con-

man at the centre storm is 48-year- rick Meehan, who eed from jail in ter serving nearly years.

judge, Lord Rob- said: "There is gal justification ver for saying Meehan was convicted."

ent on to suggest eehan's conviction ling elderly Mrs

ehan yesterday

Ross still stood, the pardon. judge spoke out at d of a second trial e same murder. time, 38-year-old addell was in the He was a prosecu- itness when Mee- a life sentence in

rday, the jury ed Waddell of — and also cleared giving false evid- Meehan's trial. ng the judge's ng up. Meehan d angrily from the gallery at Edin- High Court. said outside: "I as well tear up my pardon. It's a ss piece of paper. as I am still con-

judge said of the " In the ordinary language if you someone you par- em for something ave done—not for aing they haven't

certainly doesn't the conviction

ho killed Rachel ss?—Centre Pages.

THE GROUP IN THE BIG TV RUMPUS

Johnny Rotten, leader of the Sex Pistols, opens a can of beer. Last night their language made TV viewers froth.

When the air turned blue..

INTERVIEWER Bill Grundy introduced the Sex Pistols to viewers with the comment: "Words actually fail me about the next guests on tonight's show."

The group sang a number — and the amazing interview got under way.

GRUNDY: I am told you have received £40,000 from a record company. Doesn't that seem to be slightly opposed to an anti-materialistic way of life.

PISTOL: The more the merrier.

GRUNDY: Really.

PISTOL: Yea, yea.

GRUNDY: Tell me more then.

PISTOL: F——ing spent it, didn't we.

GRUNDY: You are serious?

PISTOL: Mmmm.

GRUNDY: Beethoven, Mozart, Bach?

PISTOL: They're wonderful people.

GRUNDY: Are they?

PISTOL: Yes they really turn us on. They do.

GRUNDY: Suppose they turn other people on?

PISTOL, (in a whisper): That's just their tough s——.

GRUNDY: It's what?

PISTOL: Nothing—a rude word. Next question.

GRUNDY: No, no. What was the rude word?

PISTOL: S——.

GRUNDY: Was it really? Good heavens. What about you girls behind? Are you married or just enjoying yourself?

GIRL: I've always wanted to meet you.

GRUNDY: Did you really? We'll meet afterwards, shall we?

PISTOL: You dirty old man. You dirty old man.

GRUNDY: Go on, you've got a long time yet. You've got another five seconds. Say something outrageous.

PISTOL: You dirty sod. You dirty bastard.

GRUNDY: Go on. Again.

PISTOL: You dirty f——er.

GRUNDY: What?

PISTOL: What a f——ing rotter

GRUNDY: Well, that's it for to-night . . . I'll be seeing you soon. I hope I'm not seeing YOU again. Goodnight.

THE FILTH AND THE FURY!

A POP group shocked millions of viewers last night with the filthiest language heard on British television.

The Sex Pistols, leaders of the new "punk rock" cult, hurled a string of four-letter obscenities at interviewer Bill Grundy on Thames TV's family teatime programme "Today".

The Thames switchboard was flooded with protests.

Nearly 200 angry viewers telephoned the Mirror. One man was so furious that he kicked in the screen of his £380 colour TV.

Grundy was immediately carpeted by his boss and will apologise in tonight's programme.

Shocker

A Thames spokesman said: "Because the programme was live, we could not foresee the language which would be used. We apologise to all viewers."

The show, screened at peak children's viewing time, turned into a shocker when Grundy asked about £40,000 that the Sex Pistols received

By STUART GREIG, MICHAEL McCARTHY and JOHN PEACOCK

from their record company.

One member of the group said: "F——ing spent it, didn't we?"

Then when Grundy asked about people who preferred Beethoven, Mozart and Bach, another Sex Pistol remarked: "That's just their tough s——"

Later Grundy told the group: "Say something outrageous."

A punk rocker replied: "You dirty sod. You dirty bastard." "Go on. Again," said Grundy.

"You dirty f——er."

"What?"

Uproar as viewers jam phone

"What a f——ing rotter As the Thames switch became jammed, viewers the Mirror to voice complaints.

Lorry driver James Ho 47, was outraged that eight-year-old son Lee h the swearing . . . and k in the screen of his T V.

"It blew up and I knocked backwards." he "But I was so angry and gusted with this filth I took a swing with my b

"I can swear with anyone, but I don't want sort of muck coming int home at teatime."

Mr. Holmes, of Beec Walk, Waltham Abbey, E added: "I am not a vi person, but I would li have got hold of Grundy

"He should be sacke encouraging this sort of gusting behaviour."

WHO ARE THESE PUNKS?

PAGE NINE

"IN SOME WAYS IT WAS OUR FINEST MOMENT, BUT IN OTHERS IT WAS THE BEGINNING OF THE END."
Jones

In Thames Television's subsequent inquest, an unnamed producer revealed that the programme's researcher, Christine Whitehead, had warned producer Mike Housego that the Pistols might use the F-word. However, the decision had been made to let the appearance continue as it was the last item on the show, with the credits imminent. Grundy was disciplined by Thames boss Jeremy Isaacs (who was later the head of Channel 4), while an internal memo informed the production team that the conduct of the interview fell far below the usual standards, referring to "inexcusably sloppy journalism". *Today* was cancelled two months later. Grundy

never worked in prime-time television again (he died in 1993, aged 69, of a heart attack).

In subsequent years, there has been much speculation – prompted by his own quip on the show – over Grundy's sobriety or otherwise, but the presenter always denied being drunk and later told *The Guardian*, "You can't do a job like I do without being sober." For his part, Rotten not only insisted that the presenter had "led the charge" at the free alcohol in the green room, but that he himself had been up for two days after taking amphetamine sulphate (the drug nicknamed "speed"). That may have impaired his judgement regarding the sobriety or otherwise of Mr Grundy, although Banshee Steve Severin has also suggested Grundy was less than stone-cold sober. Another story that's since done the rounds is that Grundy simply didn't want to interview the Pistols. He'd been the first man to interview the Beatles on TV and thought that these spiky, anarchic young reprobates were beneath him, which seems perfectly believable, especially given the large generation/cultural gap between the parties.

Whatever the truth of the presenter's condition or temperament, those 90 explosive seconds catapulted the Pistols from near unknowns who'd just started appearing in the music press to the most talked about band in the country, a group that would be adored or loathed from that moment on. For many, they were everything that pop had been lacking: fresh, exciting, unpredictable and, well, controversial. For the guardians of the nation's moral fibre, they had created a panic and became public enemy number one.

Overnight, the Pistols were dropped by EMI and almost all their gig and hotel bookings were pulled as they instantly became personae non gratae. Of the 24 gigs lined up for the subsequent

Above – British author and punk music critic Jon Savage at the San Francisco Mining Exchange, San Francisco, US, 28 August 1978.

"Anarchy Tour" just seven took place. Matlock has claimed that the police arrived at *Today* – merely moments after the band had left – wielding truncheons. Meanwhile, guitarist Jones has refuted any suspicion that the whole thing was a publicity stunt.

"I don't think it was planned," he told *Classic Rock* years later, suggesting that far from orchestrating a tabloid-worthy incident, McLaren's initial reaction had actually been one of horror until he saw the subsequent press the next day and realised the potential in controversy. The Pistols' manager admitted as such in 2007, perhaps with a slight tweak of history, telling *The Guardian*, "I knew the moment the autocue lady threw up her hands and her bag, her make-up cascading through the air, that we had smashed the deception. It was live TV, and the Sex Pistols were front-page."

England's Dreaming author Jon Savage argues that in fact the Grundy incident was very damaging for the fledgling band. "From then until their demise in January 1978, they added only four new songs to their repertoire and their approach to their audience and their music remained the same. They were flies in the amber of notoriety." Jones admitted similar sentiments in his autobiography, *Lonely Boy: Tales from a Sex Pistol:* "In some ways it was our finest moment, but in others it was the beginning of the end."

It's tantalising to wonder what might have happened had the *Today* appearance not taken place at all. Or, perhaps, whether it would have been different if the Pistols hadn't said anything outrageous, which, in fairness, would deny the provocative essence of the group. Jones has certainly pondered this. "It was one of those sparks that just went off at the right time," he told *Classic Rock*. "Maybe that was the way it was supposed to be in the overall picture. It would've been nice to progressively continue the way we were going, but I guess it just wasn't happening quickly enough. We were getting known in the *NME*, and people were starting to show up at gigs with the punk look. But the Grundy thing just took it to a whole other level." As Rotten (who now goes by his real surname, Lydon) reflected in *1977: The Bollocks Diaries*, "Suddenly it was like the whole world hated us. Which I was perfectly happy with. It meant we were doing something right."

Above – "We mean it, maan!" The Sex Pistols perform at Paradiso, Amsterdam, Netherlands, on 5 January 1977. L–R: Glen Matlock, Johnny Rotten and Steve Jones pictured during Glen Matlock's final shows with the band.

Punk mania was unleashed overnight. Over the subsequent weeks, months and years, tabloids and broadsheets would be full of punk stories, delighting or outraging their readership. Bands and record labels would form across the country and subsequently the world. Young people would start dressing a certain way and calling themselves punks. For better or worse, the Sex Pistols on *Today* was the moment punk rock broke, sealing and turbocharging the band's blaze to notoriety and infamy. After the programme, "Anarchy in the U.K." only got to No. 38, but much greater success – and more controversy – would follow. In 90 seminal seconds of unmissable television, the Sex Pistols had arrived.

"

SUDDENLY IT WAS LIKE THE WHOLE WORLD HATED US. WHICH I WAS PERFECTLY HAPPY WITH. IT MEANT WE WERE DOING SOMETHING RIGHT.

Rotten

"

fOr KIDS LiKE US, jOINING A BaND WaS AS LiKElY AS fLYINC a

They were the last people you'd expect to form a successful group.

This was because in 1975, pop's aristocracy was full of technically advanced virtuosos, road-seasoned journeymen (and it was mostly men, in those days) and comfortable singer-songwriters from leafy middle-class backgrounds. The occasional steelworker turned rock god (the Who's Roger Daltrey), or glove factory employee turned construction worker (singer Tom Jones) were the exceptions. But the traditional paths to success were music colleges and art schools, not abusive working-class backgrounds or juvenile crime.

Steve Jones admits that before he was a Sex Pistol, he had been at rock bottom financially, an abused child, a ska-listening skinhead, a peeping Tom, a joyrider, user of prostitutes, jailbird (albeit only for three weeks, for theft) and a "hardened criminal" who couldn't even play the beautiful, rare Sunbird Special he'd stolen from Mott the Hoople's guitarist, Ariel Bender. Nevertheless, a background which had rendered him virtually unemployable seems to have provided the perfect apprenticeship for becoming the Sex Pistols' guitarist.

747

Above – Keith Moon and Roger Daltrey of The Who, onstage, 1965.

Left – Ariel Bender (Luther Grosvenor) of British rock group Mott the Hoople, pictured in July 1974. The guitarist's rare Sunbird Special was stolen by Steve Jones.

Jones was born in 1955, which, as he observes in *Lonely Boy*, was the year rock 'n' roll swept across the UK. His father, a boxer, had also been a Teddy boy – one of the cult rockers who wore slicked-backed hair and Edwardian-era clothing in the 1950s and were known for their delinquent behaviour. Steve Jones's mother, Mary, was one of the much rarer Teddy girls, who had similar sartorial taste. However, having got Mary pregnant, his father had bolted. Jones had been left in Hammersmith, London, sharing a flat with his mother, grandparents and their other three children: Barry, Martin and Mary's sister, Frances. To say living conditions were cramped is putting it mildly, although after Mary met Ron Dambagella – who became Jones's stepfather – the couple decamped to Shepherd's Bush, where they lived in a basement and then later, moved to the upstairs flat of the same premises, with barely enough money to survive.

In *Lonely Boy*, Jones blames Dambagella's arrival for his festering disaffection, a feeling of being unwanted that grew much stronger when they got rid of his beloved dog, Brucie. The guitarist also discloses a disturbing and perhaps pivotal incident: that Dambagella "fiddled" with him when Mary was in hospital recovering

from a miscarriage. Jones, an undiagnosed dyslexic, began to fall behind at school, dropped back a year, spent time in a children's home and an approved school and drifted into petty crime. As he puts it in his book, "From that point I never wanted to be at home."

Years later, a therapist put his adolescent pilfering down to someone stealing his bicycle when he was 10 or 11, but the Pistols man insists he just loved the thrill and rush of lawbreaking, while the proceeds of crime came in handy. He stole model trains, bicycles, mopeds, clothes, in fact anything that brought temporary respite from life at Benbow Road. Whenever he could, he'd stay at "Cookie's", the more equable Shepherd's Bush home of his secondary-school friend Paul Cook, who later became the drummer in the band. While the pair had various mutual friends and shared interests in music and football, they were otherwise chalk and cheese, polar opposites who nevertheless bonded. Cook learned to drum by beating on biscuit tins and listening to the Glitter Band. His report at school praised his "steady work" in music, althoughit observed, with comical foresight, that "his choice of friends occasionally leads him into trouble."

Top – Thick as thieves: Jonesy and Cookie, 3 December 1976.

Bottom – Malcolm McDowell in *A Clockwork Orange*, 1971.

Opposite – "Show us a scary punk face, Glen." Glen Matlock performing at Dunstable's Queensway Hall, 21 October 1976.

Their differing backgrounds could easily have taken them in opposite directions. Cook described Jones as a "street kid from a broken home," while the latter writes in *Lonely Boy* how Cook would be "busy doing something normal like playing football after school while I'd be off peeping Tom-ing or nicking from (top London department store) Harrods warehouse." Together, though, they became glam rockers about town, hanging out on the King's Road, watching Chelsea Football Club or going to

gigs of bands such as the Kinks, the Faces or Sly and the Family Stone. Sometimes, they'd flick through Richard Allen's cult *Skinhead* series of books or go to the movies to see films such as Stanley Kubrick's hugely influential dystopian futuristic 1971 film, *A Clockwork Orange*, which was banned in the UK because its subject matter was considered dangerous enough to inspire rebellion or copycat violence – in some ways a cinematic relation to the Sex Pistols.

At this time, Jones would mostly sport clothes like those worn by his then-idol, Rod Stewart, many of them pilfered from Granny Takes a Trip, the stoner boutique in the King's Road, frequented by Mick Jagger. He even stole a coat from Faces guitarist Ron Wood's house and in his case crime did pay. He certainly always seemed to have more ready cash than Cookie, an electrical engineer at Watney's brewery. Jones had been put off working for a living after a spell in a Walls' sausage factory, where he saw terrified pigs being slaughtered. He was looking for a way out and gradually his path started to materialise.

Malcolm McLaren claimed later on that he put the Sex Pistols together primarily as a means of scamming money from record companies, and this is partially true, for they certainly pocketed record labels' huge advances. However, this is a long way from the full story. Indeed, if anyone can be said to have started the Sex Pistols, it was Warwick Nightingale. He is now a long-forgotten character who was referred to as Wally, a name that is hardly synonymous with rock legend.

Wally was a schoolfriend of Cook and Jones, and, having observed the latter's nefarious activities, made the logical suggestion: "You've nicked all that equipment. You might as well do something with it …" Which – even though Cook's first reaction (as described to Radio 5's Adrian Chiles in 2021) was "You're crazy! What? Us lot?" – wasn't a bad idea.

The embryonic band initially called themselves The Strand, after the Roxy Music song "Do the Strand". Jones sang – or rather made some sort of noises with his mouth – and Nightingale (aka Wally) played guitar, a Gibson Les Paul copy. Cook's brother-in-law, Del Noones, played bass, or rather couldn't really play it. Later, mates from the Christopher Wren School Steve Hayes (bass) and Jimmy Macken (organ) joined in with rehearsals at the Furniture Cave on the King's Road, bashing out cover versions of Faces or Small Faces numbers, with Jones doing his best impression of Rod the Mod (Rod Stewart). It was fun but the Strand were hardly set to trouble Rod the Mod et al, until they had several pivotal encounters.

Bassist Glen Matlock, the third crucial component of Britain's soon-to-be most outrageous band, was from the same side of London and was also working class, living in a "two-up, two-down" small house in Kensal Green. However, the shy only child (who was the son of a coach builder and an accounts clerk) had little in common with Cook and Jones apart from music. After passing his eleven-plus (an exam taken by English primary school children in their final year, with a pass allowing entry to a better secondary school), he'd attended St. Clement Danes grammar school, enjoying a much better education than that of all his future bandmates. However, Matlock

knew Cookie from local football and
Nightingale from their Saturday job in
McLaren's Teddy boy-influenced clothes shop,
Let It Rock, which was also frequented by Jones.
As Matlock has often put it, he was "the right
face at the right time." Formerly a ska-loving
skinhead, he also loved the Faces. "Because they
seemed like they didn't care," he told me in
2014. The Strand gigs wouldn't last that much
longer, but things were falling into place.

Malcolm McLaren, who had been born in
Stoke Newington, was a generation older than
the band members, and was an altogether
different kind of person (he died in April 2010,
aged 64). He was a dapper English gentleman,
an art student turned art collector and an
all-round catalyst, an intellectual and an
impresario. He aimed to "rescue fashion from
commodification," and he hated hippies. A
master opportunist, he was also something the
Strand really needed: a manager. After a trip to
New York in 1972, his career in music
management had begun with the camp/
aggressive glam band the New York Dolls. By
supplying the group with provocative stage
outfits and using a hammer and sickle logo to
promote them, McLaren had started to develop
the shock tactics he'd later adopt with the
Pistols. The Dolls hadn't sold many records,
though, and kept falling apart, so in May 1975
he returned to London and the clothes shop he
ran with his partner, fashion designer Vivienne
Westwood.

By the time McLaren met the members of
the Strand, Let It Rock had transformed into
subversive S&M boutique SEX (later called
Seditionaries), and McLaren glimpsed some
potential in the motley group. At least, they
were "a bit roguish, a bit mad," although they
needed a new bass player. Matlock didn't
entirely fit the bill – he was initially a guitarist
– but the fact that they all knew each other was
enough to give him an audition. A hasty run
through the Faces' "Three Button Hand Me
Down" got him in the group.

Opposite – Malcolm McLaren dressed as a Teddy boy outside his shop Let It
Rock on the King's Road, London, 14 March 1972.

Top right – McLaren's first protégés, New York Dolls. David Johansen, front,
Billy Murcia, Johnny Thunders, Arthur Kane and Sylvain Sylvain pose in a
dressing room.

Bottom right – Queen of Punk Rockers, Pamela Rooke aka Jordan at SEX
shop on the King's Road, December 1976.

"STOP PLAYING THIS SHIT AND WRITE YOUR OWN STUFF OR GET SOMETHING TOGETHER SO YOU DEFINITELY KNOW WHAT YOU'RE DOING.

McLaren

Below top – Ian Dury, idiosyncratic singer with British pub rock band Kilburn and the High Roads, Hammersmith Odeon, 1975.

Below bottom – "I'm tense and nervous and I can't relax": Talking Heads performing on New York public access show TV Party.

Early signs weren't promising, but McLaren wasn't slow in coming forward. "We was a bit naive at the time," Cook explained in Fred and Judy Vermorel's 1978 book *Sex Pistols: The Inside Story*. "Playing all these old numbers, you know, Beatles. He [McLaren] just said 'Stop playing this shit and write your own stuff or get something together so you definitely know what you're doing.' Then we decided to play all the stuff that we liked, like early Small Faces and early Who. And we picked up from there." Meanwhile, as Matlock was heading in, Nightingale was heading out, a move instigated by McLaren, who perhaps not unreasonably felt that the bespectacled youngster was too nice for his gang of neo-Dickensian miscreants. "We sort of slung Wally out," Cook admitted in *Sex Pistols: The Inside Story*. Meanwhile, Jones – whose rough Rod Stewart impersonation meant he was never going to survive as vocalist – was improving on guitar. Matlock remembered the band telling him, "You carry on playing guitar and we'll look for a singer."

The subsequent years weren't at all kind to poor Nightingale. After his father died, he became a heroin addict and died in 1996. However, he deserves a place in history. He'd founded and left a band that were three quarters fully formed just as the first signs of what would become known as punk or punk rock were starting to appear. Shorter-haired, edgier groups such as Ian Dury's pre-Blockheads band Kilburn and the High Roads and Canvey Island's killer R&B outfit Dr Feelgood were emerging at the same time, as the "pub rock" phenomenon took

live music into smaller, rowdier venues, heralding a changing wind. "Glam rock had been and gone," Matlock told me in 2015. "The big gigs at Wembley with Yes and Genesis and Jethro Tull cost a lot of money to get into, unless you were like Steve and Paul and had ways of bunking in. But none of us could relate to that stuff anyway."

Meanwhile, across the Atlantic in New York, a similar zeitgeist was emerging with the likes of the Ramones, Patti Smith, Blondie, Talking Heads and Richard Hell and the Voidoids. That band's leader, born Richard Meyers, had been in Television with Tom Verlaine and in the Heartbreakers with fellow junkie Johnny Thunders. Hell's trademark look – torn T-shirts and spiky hair – is captured on the sleeve of the seminal Voidoids single, "Blank Generation", and he was safety-pinning his clothes well before it became a British punk fashion statement.

The US groups' members mostly came from comfortable homes, in stark contrast to their impecunious British counterparts. They had relocated to New York, seeking adventure. Once there, they tapped into the city's desolate, nihilistic, hedonistic atmosphere. "New York was on the verge of bankruptcy in the mid-1970s," Studio 54 discotheque founder Ian Schrager told me for a *Guardian* piece in 2018. "Danger was in the air, people were getting mugged, but it was also a creative, bohemian time. You could really feel the energy in the gay clubs: there were frantic, intense, sweating bodies everywhere. Straight people hadn't yet learned to let it all hang out." It wasn't just New York where something was brewing. For example, Ohio bequeathed the new wave experimentalists Devo (from Akron) and Cleveland's Dead Boys, whose 1977 single "Sonic Reducer" remains a punk rock classic.

In the UK, other characters that would create the early punk scene were starting to connect. Future Clash manager (and McLaren associate) Bernard Rhodes also occasionally advised the Strand, while the would-be Pistols made friends with various SEX customers or staff. Pamela Rooke, soon to be renowned punk character "Jordan" (not to be confused with the media celebrity Katie Price, who adopted the same name), worked in the boutique, where she wielded a whip to intimidate/impress customers. She sported a peroxide beehive and wore the shop's outfits – see-through skirts with no underwear, torn tops or a leotard – in public, much to the horror of unsuspecting bystanders.

Above – An early glimpse of Blondie's Debbie Harry, performing at CBGB, New York, 1976.

Above – Dread meets punk rocker uptown: Don Letts and club promoter Andrew Czezowski outside seminal early punk club The Roxy, Covent Garden, London, 28 March 1977.

Acme Attractions, also on the King's Road, was another popular pre-punk haunt. Assistant Don Letts played dub and reggae to clientele including the Strand, future members of the Clash, *NME* reporter/future Pretenders singer/ occasional Jones squeeze Chrissie Hynde and even, when he was in London, Bob Marley. Letts subsequently played Jamaican imports to punk audiences at Covent Garden punk club, the Roxy. Something was starting to take shape. The Strand – now calling themselves Swankers – needed a singer.

Their next move, strangely enough, was to try out two potential new guitarists after Cook apparently threatened to leave unless they got someone to cover Jones's still very raw talent. Fatefully, neither *NME* writer Nick Kent nor Steve New (who'd form Rich Kids with Matlock some years later) fitted in satisfactorily and Jones was starting to get better, so in the end his Pistols job was safe.

McLaren then tried rather ambitiously and unsuccessfully to recruit Richard Hell, but in fact the solution to the vocalist problem was found much closer to home. Among the visitors to SEX were three friends, John Simon Ritchie, later infamous as Sex Pistol Sid Vicious, John Wardle, who would become "Jah Wobble", on account of how Ritchie mumbled his surname, and one John Lydon. This scruffy urchin with green hair who had "I hate …" written above the band name on his Pink Floyd T-shirt was about to become Johnny Rotten.

Cook told the *Sex Pistols: The Inside Story* authors how he'd glimpsed Lydon in the shop. "I thought he looked pretty good and I said to Malcolm to look out for this bloke. And he's come into the shop and then Malcolm must have asked him 'Do you want to sing?'"

Rather than audition Lydon in the conventional manner, they just stood him in front of the SEX jukebox, spun Alice Cooper's "I'm Eighteen" and told him to pretend he was onstage. "We thought 'He's got what we want'," Cook remembered. "Bit of a lunatic. A frontman. That's what we're after. A frontman who had definite ideas about what he wanted to do. We weren't really worried about whether he had a great voice."

In *Anger is an Energy*, Lydon admits he was "a full-on, hardcore, lunatic male," but makes the astute point that this was exactly what pop music needed. Like Hell, he wore safety pins, in his case to hold together his ripped clothes rather than as a fashion statement. Matlock thought "he just seemed the right guy to do it." McLaren realised Lydon couldn't sing and had no obvious sense of rhythm. "But he had this charm of a boy in pain, trying to pretend he's cool," he explained later. "That was the most accessible thing. You knew all the girls were gonna love him. They were like young assassins." By now the band had started calling themselves Kutie Jones and his Sex Pistols, which was shortened to the Sex Pistols when Lydon joined. Meanwhile, on account of his poor teeth, Jones rechristened their newest member "Johnny Rotten". Everything was falling into place.

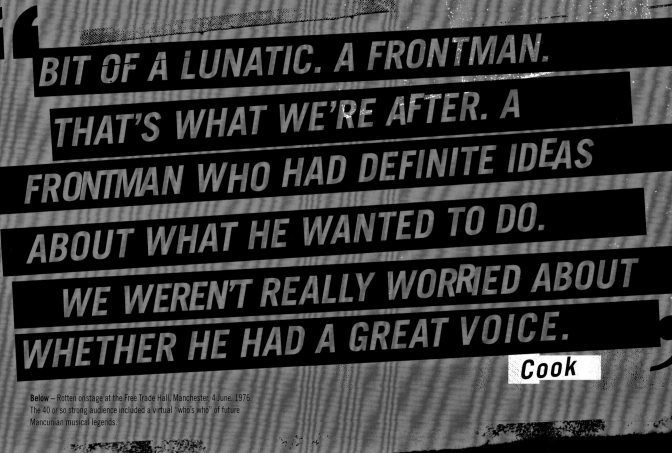

> *"BIT OF A LUNATIC. A FRONTMAN. THAT'S WHAT WE'RE AFTER. A FRONTMAN WHO HAD DEFINITE IDEAS ABOUT WHAT HE WANTED TO DO. WE WEREN'T REALLY WORRIED ABOUT WHETHER HE HAD A GREAT VOICE."*

Cook

Below – Rotten onstage at the Free Trade Hall, Manchester, 4 June, 1976. The 40 or so strong audience included a virtual "who's who" of future Mancunian musical legends.

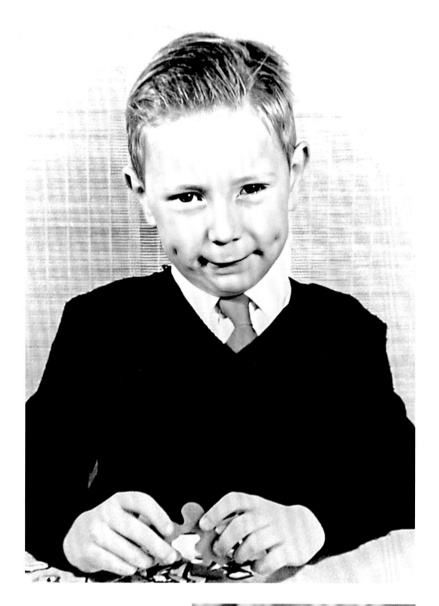

John Lydon had endured a troubled childhood. He was born on 31 January 1956, the eldest son of Irish immigrants, in Finsbury Park, north London. Lydon/Rotten's early years were also spent in confined living conditions. "In the bedroom was Mum, Dad, me, and then my younger brothers, as they arrived … Then it was six: four kids, two parents … you imagine: two double beds and a cot in a tiny room with an oil heater," Lydon wrote in *Anger is an Energy*. His mother suffered several miscarriages, and on one occasion her son was even instructed to flush the sad aftermath down the toilet (an incident which would influence the Sex Pistols song "Bodies"). As he put it, "It's quite a thing to carry a bucket of miscarriage – and you can see the little fingers and things in it – and have to flush it all down the outdoor toilet."

At the age of seven, he went into a coma after contracting spinal meningitis. When he awoke, he had lost his memory. "I didn't know who I was, my parents. I couldn't hold a spoon," he told me for *The Guardian*, explaining how he recovered through anger, which would become a key artistic drive as the period left him with a ferocious need to express himself. Meningitis had left him with a permanent, slightly manic stare, leading to him being dubbed "Johnny Dum Dum" on his return to school. He squirrelled himself away in libraries, devouring literary classics to help him to use words as weapons. Lydon attended Kingsway Princeton College of Further Education – where he met Ritchie/Vicious and made a big impression on another student, actor Timothy Spall (who later made his name in the popular TV drama/comedy *Auf Wiedersehen Pet*, and went on to become highly accomplished in a variety of roles). "In English, this guy with a Rod Stewart haircut was asking these wonderful, exciting questions about *Waiting for Godot*," he told *The Guardian* in 2021. "I remember thinking: 'This guy's bright.' He was clearly the most intelligent person in the class. That was John Lydon."

Top – "When I grow up I want to be the anti-Christ." John Lydon aka Johnny Rotten, aged 8, 1964.

Right – "It wasn't that difficult to be outrageous": Timothy Spall, 1978.

Opposite – Johnny Rotten.

Lydon hated most television and mainstream pop and mostly listened to Peter Hammill's weird prog band Van der Graaf Generator, Captain Beefheart, Can or reggae, bought from a stall under Finsbury Park Station. After briefly working for his crane driver father, he'd dyed his hair green after hacking most of his previously long locks off, an act of rebellion for which he was thrown out of the family home. As Timothy Spall remembers, "It wasn't that different to be that angry or outrageous. We were all doing it."

The difference was that Lydon channelled his feelings into a band, which seemed unattainable for kids like him. As his old mate Jah Wobble put to me in 2015, "When he told me he was joining a band called the Sex Pistols, he might as well have said he was becoming a 747 pilot, because working-class kids like us just didn't do that." But suddenly, aged 20, Rotten had the perfect vehicle for his opinions and frustrations, the Pistols, who Spall found "naughty and funny and reacted against the end of glam rock where Marc Bolan had become kind of fat."

Initially, they carried on where the Strand/ Swankers left off. Rehearsing in London's Denmark Street (at that time the London equivalent of New York's "Tin Pan Alley") where Jones often squatted in the rehearsal room, they ran through a set of covers including the Who's "Substitute", Dave Berry's R&B snarl "Don't Gimme No Lip, Child", Jonathan Richman and the Modern Lovers' proto-punk "Roadrunner" and various Small Faces songs. The Pistols' first original composition had started off as Wally Nightingale's tune "Scarface" before being completely rewritten as "Did You No Wrong". Then Matlock got the idea for "Pretty Vacant", a song which would become their third single, a Top 6 smash and a punk rock classic.

According to the bassist, McLaren had come back from the States with a poster for a Richard Hell gig with several song titles across it including "Blank Generation". "It summed up how we felt," Matlock writes in his autobiography *I Was a Teenage Sex Pistol*. "How could I express that feeling in a distinctly Sex Pistols way?"

The bassist found the answer while staring at Lydon. Thinking the singer looked "pretty awful," the bassist tried to think of a phrase that would suggest the same meaning as "Blank Generation" and came up with "Pretty Vacant". For the melody, he reworked the simple repeated octave pattern from, of all things, Abba's "SOS". Thus, one of the biggest-selling and most famous pop groups in history found themselves unwittingly becoming part of the creative process of a punk group. Meanwhile, "Pretty Vacant"'s instantly memorable chorus was loosely inspired by the Small Faces' "Wham Bam Thank You Ma'am". Not that you can hear traces of either in the finished song. Matlock wrote most of the lyrics, although Rotten swiftly replaced his not entirely epoch-defining *"If you don't like this, up yer bum, we're going down the pub"* with the infinitely superior *"Forget your cheap comments, we know we're for real."*

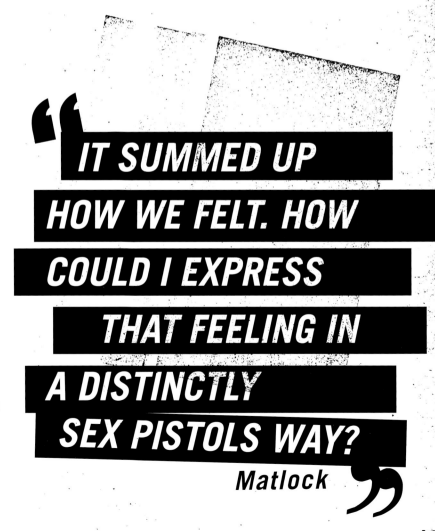

Opposite top – Bill Harkleroad aka Zoot Horn Rollo (guitar) and Captain Beefheart aka Don Van Vliet with other members of Captain Beefheart and His Magic Band c. 1970.

Opposite bottom – Van der Graaf Generator rehearsing somewhere in Wales, 1975. L to R: Hugh Banton, Peter Hammill, Guy Evans and Dave Jackson.

Above – "Going faster miles an hour": Jonathan Richman and the Modern Lovers onstage at Town Hall, New York, 17 October 1976.

" IT SUMMED UP HOW WE FELT. HOW COULD I EXPRESS THAT FEELING IN A DISTINCTLY SEX PISTOLS WAY?
Matlock "

After that, the library-educated singer opened the floodgates when it came to writing lyrics for the Pistols. One of Rotten's first, "Seventeen" (originally titled "Lazy Sod") reworked an early Jones attempt at songwriting in favour of such brutally withering putdowns as "*You're only 29, got a lot to learn, but when your mummy dies she will not return.*"

This song – subsequently a highlight of *Never Mind the Bollocks* – is an astonishingly prescient early statement of intent. "*We make noise cos it's our choice, it's what we want to do. We don't care about long hair: we don't wear flares,*" sang Lydon, his voice the essence of untamed raw vitriol. All that remained from Jones's prototype was the druggy outsider line: "*Oh I don't work, I just speed / That's all I need.*"

McLaren loved it and applied his entrepreneurial skills to maximising their songwriting talents. He issued the band with instructions that they were to write a song that would promote SEX, requesting something about bondage and S&M to play in the shop. Instead, Lydon wrote a song about an unattainable woman with lots of underwater references. Only the title – "Submission" – bore any relation to what McLaren had intended. It was a minor act of rebellion, but unbeknown to either, this was the first indication that the two men might have very differing agendas, something which would prove explosive later on. Still, they had the line-up, they had the name and now they had some songs.

> "**WE MAKE NOISE COS IT'S OUR CHOICE, IT'S WHAT WE WANT TO DO.**"
> *Lydon*

Right – "Without much controversy": Glen Matlock, Johnny Rotten and Steve Jones perform at Notre Dame Hall, London, 15 November 1976, the first of two appearances there.

THEY'RE GONNA BE BiGGeR

The Sex Pistols were ready for an audience.

Saint Martin's School of Art in Charing Cross Road, London, is famously immortalised in Pulp's hit "Common People". "She studied sculpture at Saint Martin's College …" sings Jarvis Cocker, and it really was the place where the former film studies student met the Greek art student who "had a thirst for knowledge" but "could never live like Common People". Saint Martin's hosted the Sex Pistols' first gig, a fact which is less well known than Pulp's connection with the place.

Like Cocker, Pistols bassist Glen Matlock – then aged 19 – was a St. Martin's student, and he realised that the top floor common room could provide a ready-made venue and audience of fellow students, so he organised the gig. "I had a bottle of vodka before going on and they pulled the plugs on us," he remembered to me in 2015. "People were shoving each other around. Then it all descended into chaos. I think we played half a dozen numbers, mostly covers. "Pretty Vacant" and "No Feelings" were already in the set but I don't think we got to play them." That night laid the foundations for punk in the UK, despite seemingly inauspicious beginnings for this new kind of music.

Right – Prince Charming and punk queen; Adam Ant and Jordan, backstage at the Roxy club.

BE THAN THE BEATLES

On 6 November 1975 Matlock badgered Fifties/rock 'n' roll-based act Bazooka Joe (whose bassist, Stuart Goddard, is now better known as Adam Ant) into letting the Sex Pistols support them. The college was opposite the Denmark Street rehearsal room, which meant that Jones could simply lug his bulky 100w Marshall amp over the road. Otherwise, the band turned up without equipment, hoping that the main band would let them borrow theirs.

The headliners were billed as "Bazooka Joe and his rhythm hot shots". The 20 or so people who turned up got to see the not exactly grand unveiling of one of British pop's legendary groups for an admission fee of 50p. The Pistols already looked the part even if they didn't yet sound it. Rotten wore his torn "I hate Pink Floyd" T-shirt and baggy pinstripe trousers. Cook's hair was a shorter, punkier version of a Rod Stewart spiky mop. Matlock sported crudely fetching paint-splattered trousers.

According to the bassist, McLaren plied the band with alcohol just before their performance, while Jones writes in *Lonely Boy* about how he was so nervous that he had a couple of pints and a Mandrax (sedative) to calm him down. Reports

> ## "I HAD A BOTTLE OF VODKA BEFORE GOING ON ... PEOPLE WERE SHOVING EACH OTHER AROUND. THEN IT ALL DESCENDED INTO CHAOS.
> ### Matlock "

Below — The Who — John Entwistle, Roger Daltrey, Keith Moon and Pete Townshend — perform on Dick Clark's *Where the Action Is* TV show near Tower Bridge, London, 18 March 1966.

Opposite top — Andrew Czezowski, co-founder of early punk venue The Roxy, being filmed at his home in Covent Garden, London, 1977.

Opposite bottom — The Small Faces, photographed 20 November 1965.

of what happened next vary, but it's generally accepted that the set lasted 20 minutes before Bazooka Joe pulled the plug. Rotten apparently spent much of the short gig blowing his nose into the microphone, while the set of mostly covers included the Monkees' "I'm Not Your Stepping Stone", reinvented in trademark sneering style, and the Who's "Substitute", along with Pistols' original "Seventeen". Former student Sebastian Conran's verdict on how the band went down that night eerily mirrors the reaction that would subsequently occur around the country after their gigs: a mix of adoration and sheer loathing.

"Most respected people at the college really liked it," Conran told *GQ* in 2015. "Others were really shocked and horrified, describing them as 'revolting'. As it went on it felt like some great art movement. I was unbelievably naive, as Malcolm McLaren said it was an attitude thing." Goddard/Ant later told *England's Dreaming* author Jon Savage that he'd been impressed by how the Pistols "came in as a gang. They looked like they couldn't give a fuck about anybody." Future Adam and the Ants guitarist Marco Pirroni was also in attendance, his verdict enshrined in

Stephen Colegrave and Chris Sullivan's book, *Punk*: "They were brilliant. I couldn't say musically brilliant but it was a shock to see. They were nothing like you'd ever seen before. They captured all the things you wanted to do and say … with style."

The Pistols had arrived with the beginnings of an entourage – McLaren, Westwood, Jordan, future Roxy club promoter Andy Czezowski among them – and Goddard noted how Rotten changed the lyrics of the covers. For example, the Small Faces' "Whatcha Gonna Do About It" was adapted from "I want you to know that I love you baby" to the more nihilistic "hate you baby". Meanwhile, Goddard's Bazooka Joe bandmates were so appalled they turned the sound off, leading to a scuffle as an outraged Rotten attacked their silenced equipment. By this point, though, Jones had undergone an epiphany, which presumably wasn't just down to the Mandrax.

"I remember looking at John and leaning on him for a second as we were playing," he writes in *Lonely Boy*. "He kind of pushed me away a little bit and at that moment I was thinking, 'This, right now, is the best thing in the world.'"

Above – "One day I'm gonna write one of the greatest Christmas songs ever." Shane MacGowan, early punk and future Pogue.

Opposite – "Wi-wi-wild youth": Billy Idol of Generation X performs onstage at the Marquee Club, London, September 1977.

Goddard/Ant agreed, telling Savage, "The impression left on me was total. They had a certain attitude I'd never seen, they had bollocks and a look in their eyes that said: 'We're going to be massive.'" He quit Bazooka Joe to form his own punk band the next day. Gradually, the Pistols would have that effect on many more people.

Although Rotten plays down notions that McLaren was some sort of fiendish managerial genius, the SEX boss had decided that he wanted the Pistols to be different from other groups. Not that their inexperience and generally oppositional demeanour meant they could be much else, but McLaren kept them away from the pub circuit, booking them into venues where bands didn't often play.

The short, sharp shock of the debut was followed by gigs at similar colleges, such as Holborn Central School of Art (supporting the awkwardly named Roogalator) and Hertfordshire College of Art in St Albans, where the Pistols simply turned up claiming to be the support band and were allowed to play. In the audience that

night was Shanne Hasler, who would form the Nipple Erectors with future Pogues singer Shane MacGowan, and like Goddard/Ant instantly became a fervent fan.

"They were so bad I thought it was a kind of ironic take on the Sixties and enjoyed it," she told punk77 website in 2001. "We danced and mucked around. I was wearing an old lady's salmon pink corset from Oxfam, a holster with two guns, ripped tights and outsize ice-skating boots. I just happened to have bright orange home butchered hair due to a henna/peroxide chemical reaction." Shortly afterwards she picked up a bass – an early example of how punk opened musical doors for women in what had always been a hugely male-dominated music scene. All such developments were sowing tiny seeds.

In 2014, former National College of Food Technology student Simon Wright told *The Guardian* how he became a convert after seeing the Pistols play the establishment in Weybridge in November 1975. "Malcolm McLaren had been booking them into obscure colleges outside London to get them some live experience," he

"THE IMPRESSION LEFT ON ME WAS TOTAL. THEY HAD A CERTAIN ATTITUDE I'D NEVER SEEN, THEY HAD BOLLOCKS.

Adam Ant "

remembered. "They basically emptied the hall. There were about five of us left at the end of the gig and it was the best thing I'd ever seen."

After just a few gigs in 1975 – others included Westfield College and the Queen Elizabeth College, both in London – the Pistols had a small but visually distinctive following, and were further boosted by their first ever mention in the music press. *NME* (*New Musical Express*) reviewer Kate Phillips declared, "They're going to be the Next Big Thing, or maybe the Next Big Thing After That," after the show at the Queen Elizabeth, despite having missed the whole performance.

By the time of the Ravensbourne College, Chislehurst gig on 9 December, future *Never Mind the Bollocks* classics "Pretty Vacant", "New York" and "Submission" were all featuring in the setlist, while the band's following included "Bromley Contingent" faces Susan Ballion and William Broad, now better known as Siouxsie Sioux and Billy Idol. As usual, not everyone was impressed. In 2002, music journalist Nigel Williamson remembered the Ravensbourne show – admission 50p – in *The Guardian* and admitted that he wished he'd stayed in the pub. "The Sex Pistols can barely play their instruments," he moaned. "Each tuneless thrash that passes for a song sounds the same as the one before. And while the spotty, under-nourished frontman knows how to sneer, he certainly doesn't know how to sing." Mind you, Williamson wasn't any

Above – "Punk definitely influenced me": Paul Weller and the Jam perform at punk club The Roxy, Covent Garden, London, 24 February 1977. L–R Weller, Rick Buckler, Bruce Foxton.

Opposite – Gravedigger turned Damned singer Dave Vanian and girlfriend (c. 1977).

more taken by an early glimpse of the now equally legendary the Jam, declaring that: "They are almost worse than the Sex Pistols and we ask for our money back."

The Pistols might have been first out of the traps, but the likes of the Jam weren't that far behind them. Builder's son and Who fan Paul Weller had started his Woking-based outfit in 1972, adding fellow Sheerwater High School pupils Rick Buckler (drums) and Bruce Foxton (bass, backing vocals) to form the classic line-up. The Jam were never really a punk group, but their short, spiky haircuts and Weller's archetypal "angry young man" (referring to John Osborne's Fifties play *Look Back in Anger*, that established the concept of a cynical and world-weary young male protagonist who is irredeemably furious and resentful) stance certainly endeared them to punk audiences. "We already had our look, but the punk thing definitely influenced me," Weller told Radio 4's *Mastertapes* in 2021. "Punk was important for people of my age, because it was our time. We were too young to be part of the Sixties scene, and there was nothing really much in the Seventies. Maybe Bolan and Bowie in the early Seventies. But by the mid-Seventies it was really dull. There was no one singing for us and representing us."

The provocatively named London SS were a band managed by McLaren associate Bernard Rhodes (after the pair fell out) and they rehearsed in 1975. They never played a gig, but guitarist Mick Jones went on to form the Clash – who recorded London SS song "1-2, Crush on You" – and bassist Tony James started Generation X with Billy Idol. Other London SS members included future Clash bassist and drummer Paul Simonon and Terry Chimes, while second Clash drummer Nicky "Topper" Headon occupied their drum stool for a week. Amongst other briefly flickering bands at this stage was the cheekily named Masters of the Backside. Their line-up consisted of future Pretenders singer Chrissie Hynde along with Hammer horror obsessed Dave Vanian, Captain Sensible and Rat Scabies, a bunch of gravediggers and toilet cleaners who (along with Brian James) would metamorphose into the Damned. Meanwhile, the fluctuating Flowers of Romance line-up variously included future members of the Clash and Public Image

"WE'RE NOT INTO MUSIC. WE'RE INTO CHAOS."
Jones

Ltd (guitarist Keith Levene), the Slits (Viv Albertine and Palmolive), Siouxsie and the Banshees (drummer Kenny Morris) and Adam and the Ants (Marco Pirroni). Meanwhile, their short-lived drummer was one Sid Vicious, and the band name had been suggested by none other than Johnny Rotten.

The Pistols singer's own group started 1976 in much the same way as they'd ended 1975: at the forefront of an organic music revolution, and with anarchy and ringing eardrums in their wake. Matlock declared it "was for the dissatisfied youth from the dissatisfied youth. Everyone was looking for something. Everybody knew exactly what they didn't want but didn't know what they did want. When we arrived on the scene … it was what we had been looking for, but never knew we needed."

After more low-key gigs, two performances in February 1976 were considerably more significant. First, on 12 February, they supported the new wave-ish Eddie and the Hot Rods at the Marquee Club in Wardour Street, which was renowned as a platform for rising stars. Acts who'd trodden the Wardour Street boards before Rotten and pals included the Rolling Stones, the Who, Pink Floyd, Led Zeppelin and Queen – ironically all groups the Pistols sought to overthrow, although the Who's vitriolic anti-class system "Substitute" was still in the live set. The Marquee gig was attended by EMI's Mike Thorne, who told the venue's website years later that the Pistols were "immediate and challenging", and *NME*'s Neil Spencer, who gave the band their first proper live review.

At five decades' distance, Spencer's verdict – published in the issue dated 21 February 1976 – looks incredibly prophetic. "Don't look over your shoulder, the Sex Pistols are coming," declared the headline. There were only about 20 people there when the Pistols were on and Spencer only caught the last few numbers but

that was enough for him to hail, "A quartet of spiky teenage misfits from the wrong side of various London roads, playing 60s styled white punk rock … Punks? Springsteen, Bruce and the rest of them would be shredded if they went up against these boys. They've played less than a dozen gigs as yet, have a small but frantic following, and don't get asked back."

According to the paper's gossip column the following week, the band were thrown off the rest of Eddie and the Hot Rods' tour because Rotten had kicked a chair into the Marquee crowd, apparently as a result of the onstage monitors being turned off, just as had happened at that first gig with Bazooka Joe.

That first review also included a famous Pistols quote – credited to an unidentified Jones, who'd surely been primed by McLaren: "We're not into music. We're into chaos." In those days, when such music weeklies as *NME* shifted hundreds of thousands of copies, such coverage was essentially a free advert to a potentially massive audience.

The first use of the word "punk" in conjunction with the Pistols was almost certainly included in Spencer's review. The term had originated in the US as street slang for a hoodlum or inferior person, although it was first applied to music as long ago as 1899, when a *San Francisco Call* reporter referred to "the most punk song heard in the hall." The word started to appear in music journalism in the late 1960s and early 1970s. In 1970, Ed Sanders, formerly of The Fugs, described his first solo album as "punk rock." Journalist Lester Bangs called Detroit garage rock upstarts Iggy Pop and the MC5 "punks". In March 1971, *Creem*'s Greg Shaw described The Shadows of the Knight as "hard-edged punk," while the same publication's editor Dave Marsh used the term "punk rock" in a review of ? and the Mysterians. The Ramones were singing "Judy is a Punk" in 1974.

Opposite top – The Slits, minus a bass player, in Daventry Street, London, 1977. L–R singer Ari Up (Ariane Forster, 1962 – 2010), drummer Palmolive (Paloma Romero) and guitarist Kate Korus.

Opposite bottom – "Do anything you wanna do": Eddie and the Hot Rods.

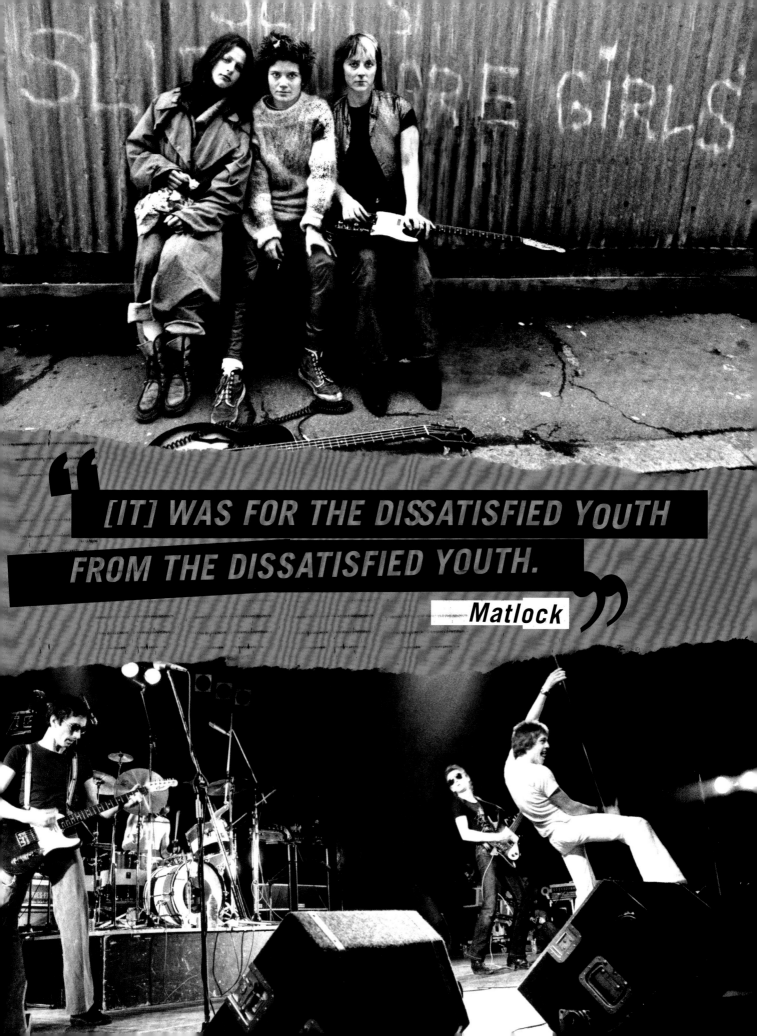

"[IT] WAS FOR THE DISSATISFIED YOUTH FROM THE DISSATISFIED YOUTH."

Matlock

Page 54 – Sex Pistols arrive for a press conference at EMI offices, in the aftermath of the *Today* programme. Manager Malcolm McLaren, 29, defended the group and claimed that they were "set up" by interviewer Bill Grundy.

Page 55 – Johnny Rotten in one of the few hotels that allowed the Pistols to stay, during the "Anarchy Tour", 1976.

Above – English artist Andrew Logan, the founder and host of the Alternative Miss World Competition, at the Grand Hall, Kensington Olympia, London on 2 October 1981.

In 1975, New York-based Legs McNeil had set up *PUNK* magazine, which covered the bands emerging at CBGB and Max's Kansas City. In May 1976, three months after Spencer used the term in the UK, *Time Out* magazine described the Pistols as playing "a mixture of Anglo-American teen/punk classics" while *Creem* man Shaw reviewed the Pistols at the 100 Club as "tortured punk rock." The term would become associated with the UK scene after journalist Caroline Coon, who briefly managed the Clash, referred to a "movement" of "third generation punks" in *Melody Maker* in August 1976. The P-word subsequently became attached and entwined with the Pistols, their music and their audience … but all that was yet to come.

On 14 February, the band played another significant show – a Valentine's Day ball at Andrew Logan's studio at Butler's Wharf on the South Bank of the Thames, which introduced them to a very different cognoscenti. Today, Logan is a well-known artist and sculptor. Back then, he was best known as the founder of the "pansexual beauty pageant" *Alternative Miss World*. Having given his first party with a record player when he was 14, he'd progressed to the heart of London's bohemian party scene. "I just loved giving parties," he remembers today. "You could just create these wonderful events. Things happened very quickly and much more organically in those days." McLaren and Westwood came to Logan's parties, so knew that the studio was a ready-made venue. "Malcolm phoned me up because he knew I had a stage," Logan, now in his seventies, remembers. "It was 2,000 square feet on the sixth floor. A perfect place."

Derek Jarman had shot a scene for his film *Sebastiane* there, and part of the set remained in the building. The floor was painted pink marble. Logan had recently designed a roof garden for the Biba superstore (a large London fashion store and famous symbol of the Swinging Sixties), purchasing a castle from their toy department and installing it in the space. "I had a bar and I'd bought a Portakabin for fifty quid and lined it in gold. It was called 'the gold room.'"

Logan still vividly remembers McLaren excitedly telling him, "'I've got this band. They're gonna be bigger than the Beatles!' I said, 'Oh how lovely,'" he chuckles. "He asked if they could play. 'Of course!' I'd always been open. That's what the alternative world is … Simply very open."

As Logan remembers it, the evening started off conventionally. People milled around, there was some music. "And Michael, my other half, had just bought a wonderful Bang & Olufsen television, and they started a row over the top of the TV and were pushing each other. Michael asked Vivienne, 'Can you be careful of my television' and she said, 'You bourgeois twit!' It was very funny." At which point the Pistols started to play.

Above – Manager Malcolm McLaren and designer Vivienne Westwood in defiant mood outside Bow Street Magistrate's Court, after being remanded on bail for fighting, June 1977.

"THEY WERE BRILLIANT. I COULDN'T SAY MUSICALLY BRILLIANT BUT IT WAS A SHOCK TO SEE. THEY WERE NOTHING LIKE YOU'D EVER SEEN BEFORE.

Marco Pirroni

"Well …" he chuckles, pausing for dramatic effect. "The building had a corrugated roof, 30 feet high. So can you imagine that sound, to people hearing them for the first time. The whole roof reverberated like a drum. 'Whoooooooo!' It was just so noisy. We all just took one look and ran into the gold room. Left out there were Jordan, baring her bosom, Vivienne and a few groupies, and that was it. We certainly heard it in the gold room, even then. It was deafening because of the roof."

In 2015, Jordan told *Mojo* that she had bared her breasts because McLaren had spotted *NME*'s Nick Kent and urged, "Take your clothes off!" to create a story. "In the middle of Iggy Pop's "No Fun", John broke all the zips on my leotard," she remembered. "I was so fed up about that, I took the back off and it went zoom."

Although Logan isn't certain, the band are believed to have played around a dozen songs, including new addition "Problems", which would appear on *Never Mind the Bollocks*. Jarman filmed at least some of the gig and his

footage – the first of the Pistols live – recently surfaced on YouTube. The sound is from a different gig, and the film itself is very grainy, but it's a piece of history.

"At that time in London there wasn't a club scene," Logan observes. "The licensing laws hadn't changed so you lived in a house, you went to work and you went to the pub. That was it. So you could create these wonderful events and news just spread like wildfire."

Others in attendance that night included Helen Wellington-Lloyd, a friend of McLaren's who would later devise the Pistols' ransom note artwork lettering, the Bromley Contingent's Simon "Boy" Barker and photographer Joe Stevens, whose pictures appeared in the music press the following week. One even made it into *The Sunday Times* magazine, alongside a playful Logan quote about how the guests had been "a mixture of lorry drivers, construction workers and philosophers." Some of these early gigs might have been a cross between a radical art "happening", an Ealing comedy and a bloody awful row.

Opposite top – Punk rock summit! Johnny Rotten with Mark Perry of *Sniffin' Glue* fanzine. *NME*'s Nick Kent in background, the Roxy, London, 1976.

Opposite bottom – "You're not going out dressed like that?!": Clothing from Seditionaries on King's Road, London, modelled by Jordan, 18 May 1977.

AN HONEST PRIMAL SCREAM

The Sex Pistols were getting noticed.

Opposite left – Stephen Morrissey.

Opposite right – Bernard Sumner performing with English punk band Warsaw, at Rafters nightclub in Oxford Street, Manchester, 30 June 1977. The band changed their name to Joy Division the following year.

In 1976, the Sex Pistols had not yet released a record, yet they were managing to inspire others to the punk cause. This had taken some doing. The February *NME* review of the Marquee gig was enough to tempt Bolton-based art student Howard Trafford to try to get to their next gig. Unfortunately for him, that booking was in High Wycombe, 200 miles away. Still, as luck would have it, Trafford had use of a teacher flatmate's little Renault for the weekend as long as he picked it up from the garage where it was being serviced. "I don't think she meant that I could drive to London," he told me in 2008. His grin suggested he still couldn't quite believe how access to that little Renault had subsequently changed his life.

On the day of the High Wycombe gig, Trafford's mate Peter McNeish was due to go to London for a student conference and had been granted travel expenses, which took care of the cost of the petrol for the Renault. "It needed all those elements to come together," Trafford explained. "But it shows how desperate we were – for something." Which they found in the Sex

Pistols. The High Wycombe show supporting Screaming Lord Sutch was, by all accounts, a thrilling, uproarious yet rather fractious affair, which ended with Rotten smashing the malfunctioning microphone into the floor. By then, Trafford and McNeish had seen enough to want to bring punk north to Manchester.

They approached McLaren, offering to organise a Pistols gig. The resulting concert, at the Lesser Free Trade Hall on 4 June 1976 (admission 50p), was attended by under 40 people, but among the audience were Stephen Morrissey, who formed the Smiths, and future Joy Division members Peter Hook and Bernard Sumner. "What the Pistols were doing made it achievable for us, working-class guys who didn't seem to have a future and weren't musicians," Sumner told me in 2019. After that 1976 gig, 17-year-old Morrissey penned a letter to *NME* favourably comparing the Pistols to the New York Dolls and cheekily saying he'd love them to become successful because "maybe then they will be able to afford some clothes which don't look as though they've been slept in."

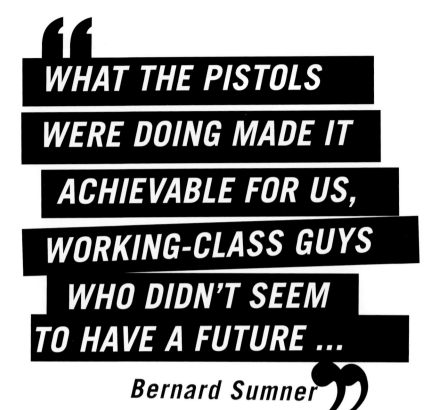

" WHAT THE PISTOLS WERE DOING MADE IT ACHIEVABLE FOR US, WORKING-CLASS GUYS WHO DIDN'T SEEM TO HAVE A FUTURE ...

Bernard Sumner "

buzzcocks

spiral scratch

By the time the Pistols returned to the venue on 20 July, the audience was much bigger. Trafford and McNeish changed their names to Howard Devoto and Pete Shelley respectively and named their own embryonic band Buzzcocks in time to offer their services as Pistols support group (they were listed bottom of the bill under Wythenshawe Bowie fans Slaughter and the Dogs). Few of the punters paying the £1 admission that night could have possibly guessed that Buzzcocks, a spiky, frenetic four-piece band with a schoolboy drummer (16-year-old John Maher) would become one of UK punk's most seminal artists.

The quartet, managed by Richard Boon, would release the movement's first DIY single (the *Spiral Scratch* EP) and influence everybody from the Smiths to Nirvana to R.E.M. Although countless people now claim to have been at that second Manchester Pistols gig – enough to inspire a book, David Nolan's *I Swear I Was There*, which

tried to uncover the truth – those definitely in attendance included future Joy Division singer Ian Curtis, Mark E. Smith, who formed the Fall, Mick Hucknall, whose punk-era band the Frantic Elevators never became stars, but whose group Simply Red did, future Cult guitarist Billy Duffy and Granada TV presenter Tony Wilson, who booked the Pistols for *So It Goes*. Wilson also set up Factory Records, the legendary label behind Joy Division, New Order and Happy Mondays. John Cooper Clarke, who became the punk poet dubbed the "Bard of Salford", said that "the gig couldn't have been a better introduction to the punk phenomenon."

The Pistols supported Joe Strummer's pub rock band, the 101ers, at the Nashville Rooms in London on 3 and 23 April, again wearing what had become a trademark look of SEX T-shirts, "brothel creeper" shoes (big chunky shoes with thick crepe soles and suede uppers) and homemade painted

Opposite top – The record that invented indie rock: *Spiral Scratch* EP by Buzzcocks.

Opposite bottom – They brought punk to Manchester … Singer Howard Devoto, drummer John Maher, bassist Steve Diggle and guitarist Pete Shelley of English punk band the Buzzcocks, *c.* early 1977.

Top left – "White crap that talks back": Mark E. Smith of the Fall.

Top right – "The bard of Salford": punk poet John Cooper Clarke with a dice in his mouth in the CBS Records photo studio, London, *c.* 1977.

Bottom – Tony Wilson, Factory Records boss, posed on set of *So It Goes* TV show.

trousers, and this engendered even more interest. While no more than a dozen people watched, among them was Strummer. Years later, he told biographer Chris Salewicz that the Pistols had been "a million miles ahead" of his own band, admitting, "I realised immediately we were going nowhere."

Legend has it that Strummer quit the 101ers to start the Clash there and then, but as ever where mythology is involved, the truth is slightly more prosaic. It was in fact several weeks later, after the Pistols played at the 100 Club, that Bernard Rhodes invited Strummer to meet Mick Jones, Keith Levene and Paul Simonen, who would – alongside drummer Terry Chimes – form the first Clash line-up. Punk's yin to the Pistols yang, or vice versa, they made their debut supporting the latter at the Black Swan pub in Sheffield on 4 July. Some months later, 101ers drummer Richard "Snakehips" Dudanski saw Strummer's new band live and could scarcely believe the transformation. "He wasn't Joe any more, he was someone else," he reflected to *Uncut*'s Allan Jones years later, referring to the singer's metamorphosis from a rockabilly type to high octane punk rocker. "His identity had changed entirely. I just thought, 'What happened to this guy?'" The effect the Pistols had on

Trafford, McNeish and Strummer would soon be replicated up and down the country.

On the south coast on 3 July, young Marianne Elliott-Said saw the Pistols play to a near-empty hall on Hastings pier, but that was enough to inspire her to start her band, X-Ray Spex. "They had drainpipes, shortish hair, and played covers," she told me in 2011, remembering the gig (also attended by future comedienne Jo Brand) where the Pistols had been booked to support rock band Budgie and paid £20. "But they must have had something because I thought, 'I can do that!'"

Elliott-Said changed her name to Poly Styrene, yelled "Oh Bondage Up Yours!" about both the sexual practice and the patriarchal society, and sang mostly fast and always astonishingly prescient songs about the consumer society and the environment. As a British-Somali woman who wore dental braces, she wonderfully rein-vented what a female singer/frontperson could look and sound like, inspiring generations of others to similarly reject tired old stereotypes.

"Before punk, there were very few women in bands and most were singers," X-Ray Spex saxophonist, Susan Whitby, aka Lora Logic, told me in 2001. "Punk opened the doors for loads of girls, Siouxsie, the Slits (fronted by 14-year-old Ari Up), the Raincoats, Gaye Advert ... Every-

Above – The Clash pictured before performing at the Belle Vue in Manchester, 15 November 1977. L-R Topper Headon, Joe Strummer, Paul Simonon and Mick Jones.

Opposite top – Proud "one chord wonders": The Adverts. L–R Laurie Driver, T.V. Smith, Gaye Advert and Howard Pickup.

Opposite bottom – "Before punk, there were few women in bands": Lora Logic and Poly Styrene of punk band X-Ray Spex, performing onstage at one of their first gigs at the Roxy, London, 11 March 1977.

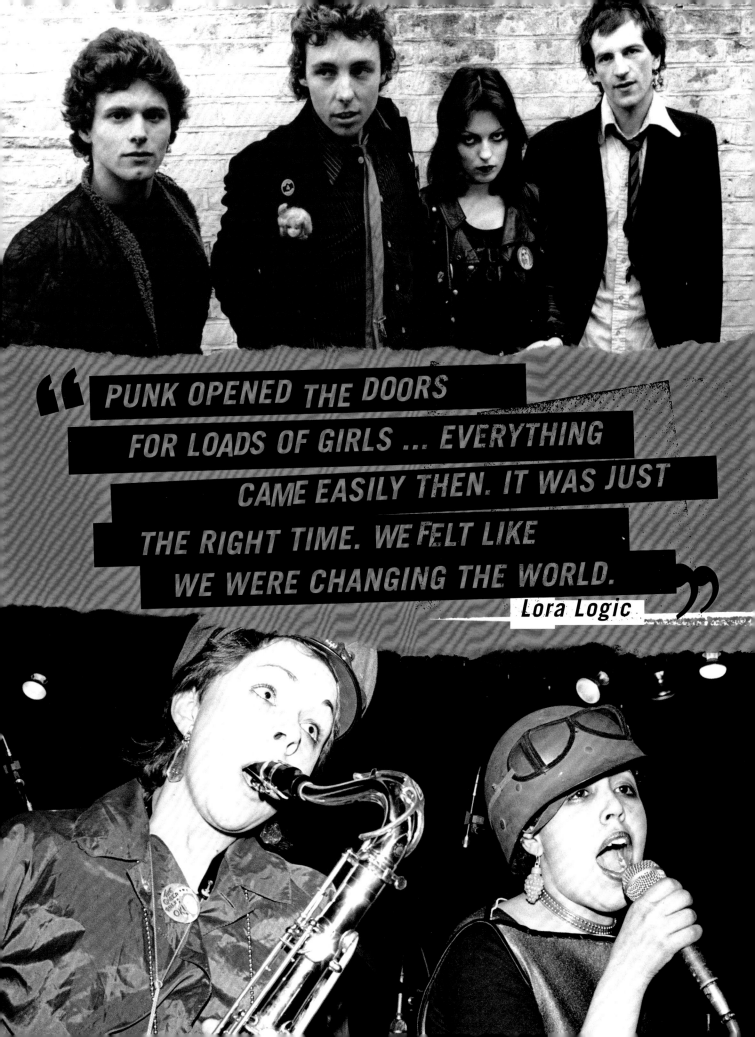

" PUNK OPENED THE DOORS FOR LOADS OF GIRLS ... EVERYTHING CAME EASILY THEN. IT WAS JUST THE RIGHT TIME. WE FELT LIKE WE WERE CHANGING THE WORLD. "

Lora Logic

> # "THEY WERE A SPECTACLE AND SEEMED TO CHALLENGE EVERYTHING YOU THOUGHT. I WAS ATTRACTED AND REPELLED."
>
> ## Jon Savage

thing came easily then. It was just the right time. We felt like we were changing the world. We used to wear dresses with breakfast plates on covered in ketchup and our perception of the world was expressed through the clothes. You'd go on a bus dressed like that and watch how people stared at you, even down the King's Road."

The aforementioned Gaye Advert (real name Gaye Black) was another south coast convert and formed the Adverts with fellow Devon ex-pat T.V. (Timothy) Smith, who'd also fled to London. Female bassists were still a very rare breed, the role having been pioneered during the glam rock era by leather clad singer-bassist Suzi Quatro, but Advert's smouldering looks and black leather image made her a punk rock pin-up. The band's songs – "One Chord Wonders", "Bored Teenagers", "No Time to Be 21" and the like – remain classics of punk's youthful energy and frustration.

Woking youngster Paul Weller – another suburban kid, as were Siouxsie and Billy Idol – saw the Pistols support old Sixties band the Pretty Things at London's Roundhouse in 1976 and wanted in. "I just thought 'This is it. This is our moment,'" he told Radio 4's *Mastertapes* in 2021. "It was our generation's time. Punk was the catalyst. I was already writing, but it shaped how I thought about songwriting."

Hearing the Pistols and then especially the Clash, who were "writing songs about what was going on" led Weller into social commentary and political songs. After notoriously initially saying he would vote Conservative (the UK party that

supports right-wing, traditional values), his politics rocketed leftward after the Jam toured the impoverished regions, and he penned "A Town Called Malice". Change was in the ether.

"In 1975, everything was shit," writer Jon Savage told me for a punk piece in *The Guardian* in 2001. "London looked like a rubbish tip, the clothes were disgusting and everybody was listening to Abba and the Carpenters, and all that stuff that is retrospectively fashionable. The *NME* was promoting these awful groups like Racing Cars. In 1976, the first Ramones album became the Holy Bible. It was obvious that soon there would be people in Britain making that kind of noise. I saw the Clash at the Fulham Town Hall and I was stunned. At that point I was completely alienated and felt very angry about everything. Then I saw the Pistols and they became more challenging on every level. They were a spectacle and seemed to challenge everything you thought. I was attracted and repelled."

By now, the music press were starting to take more notice. In April, the Ramones released their first album (including "Judy is a Punk") and the Pistols were interviewed for the first time. *Sounds'* Jonh Ingham (who'd reviewed them at El Paradise, a Soho strip club, and been intrigued by the lyrics) now met the band in the Cambridge pub in Soho and penned an article titled "The Sex Pistols are four months old" (which they were in terms of live performance). Much of the 2000-word article concerned itself with the gig, but the interview within had the beginnings of a manifes-

Opposite – Johnny Rotten and Steve Jones, about 1977.

to. "I hate hippies and what they stand for," Johnny Rotten – he of the "I hate Pink Floyd" T-shirt – declared, taking aim at pop's old guard. "I hate long hair. I hate pub bands. I want to change it so there are rock bands like us. I'm against people who just complain about *Top of the Pops* and don't do anything. I want people to go out and start something, to see us and start something, or else I'm just wasting my time."

Others feeling similarly included singer Toyah Willcox, who saw the Pistols at Bogart's, Birmingham, in September 1976. "It was fantastic," she told me. "I'd already dyed my hair bright pink and I was wearing bin-liners, because I couldn't afford clothes. I'd been ridiculed for the way I looked, but I walked into this club and suddenly I wasn't alone anymore." The early scene was hardly the height of glamour. In Whitby on 11 September, the Pistols played upstairs in a working men's club, hilariously billed as *Saturday Night Disco Featuring Top Band Sex Pistols* and were pulled off after under 20 minutes because they were drowning out the bingo a floor below. Still, judging from internet testimonies, the handful that saw the brief performance knew they'd witnessed something special.

Opposite — Toyah Willcox, 15 August 1978.

Above — The Sex Pistols perform at the 100 Club in London. L–R Steve Jones, Johnny Rotten, Glen Matlock.

There's no record of the Pistols playing Blackpool in the 1970s, but Rotten's memory seems reliable enough and in a 2012 interview for *The Guardian,* the singer told me how he admired the town's "working-class, couldn't-care-less sensibility. It's just very hard to deal with the drunken women. 'Hello, do you know I've got no knickers on?' Yes, I do." He went on to explain that Cilla Black had a residency in the town, and on her day off they'd got a gig and used her dressing room. "There was a pair of tights there so I put them over the microphone and sang the whole gig through Cilla Black's tights. If she wants a full re-enactment, I'm available."

On 19 May, County Durham-based Pauline Murray saw the soon-to-be-seminal band playing to just 10 people in the unlikely confines of Sayers nightclub in Northallerton, North Yorkshire, which usually hosted nostalgia bands such as Sixties hitmakers Wayne Fontana and the Mindbenders. After that gig, Murray and boyfriend Robert Blamire started Penetration, becoming part of a wider wave. "Suddenly, bands were more accessible," remembers Gary Nattrass,

who saw Penetration play Newcastle's Mayfair venue when he was a teenager based in Morpeth. He ended up talking to the band in their dressing room afterwards, saying it was something "which would never have happened with bands like Pink Floyd or Yes." Nattrass adopted the pseudonym Johnny Condom and formed north-east punk band the Coils. For so many working-class kids around the country, punk offered them their first chance to do something of their own, whether it was to try and seize a different future (as had Cook, Rotten, Jones and Matlock) or just register a sense of disaffection or rebellion.

"The kids at the time had been fed propaganda like 'I was in the war for you,'" Sham 69 singer Jimmy Pursey told me in 2001. "After leaving school we didn't have career opportunities and it just came to a head. Punk was an honest primal scream." The bands already spanned a spectrum of musical virtuosity, social class and age, with middle-class art school types Wire at one end and snotty-nosed upstarts Eater (whose youngest member was just 14) at the other. That band – fronted by Anglo-Egyptian Ashruf Radwan aka

SNIFFIN' GLUE...
...OTHER ROCK'n'ROLL HABITS, FOR
...NCH OF BLEEDIN' IDIOTS! ⑤ NOVEMBER '76.

Andy Blade – were formed by four Finchley schoolfriends and made a splash in 1977, especially after appearing on early punk live compilation, *The Roxy London WC2*. Suddenly, forming a successful band seemed within reach to anybody and everybody. Not everyone was impressed, mind. Disenchanted *NME* reader Neil Tennant wrote a grumbly missive to the magazine's letters page after watching Rotten (who he dubbed "El Dementoid") and band-mates get involved in a fracas with the audience at the Nashville (which Matlock subsequently explained they'd actually been trying to stop). While the Pet Shop Boys (the band Tennant went on to form) are not audibly influenced by the Pistols or punk rock, countless others were taking heed of Joe Strummer's famous battle cry of "Anyone can do it!" Helpfully, in the wake of

Mark Perry's *Sniffin' Glue and Other Rock 'n' Roll Habits*, numerous other punk fanzines emerged to help the process. *Sideburns*, a fanzine primarily dedicated to the increasingly popular band the Stranglers, even printed a picture of three guitar chords with the instruction: "Now form a band."

Meanwhile, the Pistols' TV appearance on *So It Goes* was the first time many heard "Anarchy in the U.K.", which had only been added to the setlist two weeks earlier at Birmingham Barbarella's (a small club later synonymous with Duran Duran). Rotten penned the lyrics of the seminal genera-tional anthem "almost spontaneously" in rehearsals – a volcanic eruption after years of pent-up frustration. "What Robin Williams described as 'overflowing madness'," he explained when I interviewed him for *The Guardian* in 2018. "Mix that with a bit of James Joyce and out it comes.

Above – A pile of punk fanzines, 1977, including such highly desirable titles as *Ghast Up*, *Negative Reaction*, *Gheusi and Friends*, *Situation 3*, *Viva La Resistance*, *White Stuff 2*, *Sniffin' Glue*, *Trash '77*, *Live-Wire*, *London's Burning*, and last but not least, *Skum*.

Pages 74–75 – Sex Pistols (somewhere in France).

Repression, anti-Irish racism, the belief that class was all important ... I'd seen what was coming: Ikea-made shopping centres, the destruction of personality. I was lucky to have words to express what a lot of people were feeling."

The (in)famous, boundary-busting opener – "*I am an anti-christ / I am an anarchist*" – partly reflected his Catholic schooling. "You either believe that nonsense or have something to say about it," he said. "Hopefully maliciously, because that's where the fun is." It's debatable which was the more confrontational – "*anti-christ*", with its connotations of Beelzebub or the harbinger of doom, or "*anarchist*", the ultimate rejection of political or indeed any kind of authority.

Days after showcasing this aural bombshell on regional teatime telly, Cook quit his day job, to his workmates' disbelief – it had been "a job for a lifetime, if you wanted it". And what he later described as "the best decision I ever made" took a step closer to paying off when the Pistols appeared on the cover of *Melody Maker*. Not that the band were themselves involved. Caroline Coon's cover story asked, "Punk rock: crucial or phoney?" while the inner headline branded the Pistols "Rebels against the system." Coon was a veteran of several Pistols gigs and in lieu of an interview penned a 1400-word essay analysing the band and the emerging movement behind them, paying particular attention to punk's antipathy to everything else which was going on.

"The band play exciting, hard, basic punk rock," she wrote, "but more than that, Johnny is the elected generalissimo of a new cultural movement scything through the grassroots disenchantment with the present state of mainstream rock. You need look no further than the letters pages of any *Melody Maker* to see that fans no longer silently accept the disdain with which their heroes, the rock giants, treat them. They feel deserted. Millionaire rock stars are no longer part of the brotherly rock fraternity that helped create them in the first place. Rock was meant to be a joyous celebration; the inability to see the stars or to play the music of those you can see is making a whole generation of rock fans feel depressingly inadequate."

For Coon and many others who were similarly "frustrated, bored and betrayed", the Pistols presented great white hopes, as she says, "who have decided to ignore what they believe to be the elitist pretensions of their heroes, who no longer play the music they want to hear. The Pistols are playing the music they want to hear. They are the tip of an iceberg." Which was getting bigger by the day. Coon went on to observe how bands such as the Clash, the Jam, Buzzcocks, the Damned, the Suburban Studs and Slaughter and the Dogs were all playing music that was "loud, raucous and beyond considerations of taste and finesse. As Mick Jones of the Clash says: 'It's wonderfully vital.'" Days later, Coon was on hand to report on the Pistols' first gig abroad, at the Club Du Chalet De Lac in Paris, attended by the "Bromley Contingent", and which saw Rotten wear a bondage outfit. The effect on the audience was a mix of "unrestrained enjoyment and intense hatred."

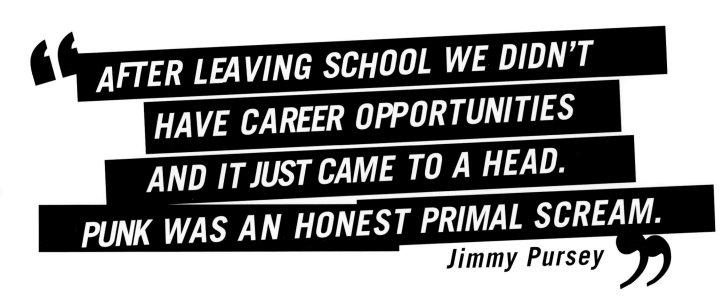

"AFTER LEAVING SCHOOL WE DIDN'T HAVE CAREER OPPORTUNITIES AND IT JUST CAME TO A HEAD. PUNK WAS AN HONEST PRIMAL SCREAM.
Jimmy Pursey"

MOST OF THESE
WOULD BE IMPRO
SUDDEN DEATH

THE SCREEN ON THE GREEN
PRESENTS A MIDNIGHT SPECIAL

"ON STAGE"

SUNDAY AUG 29TH
MIDNIGHT — DAWN

SEX PISTOLS

+ CLASH

+ BUZZCOCKS

REFRESHMENTS AVAILABLE

TICKETS £1
FROM 'SEX' 430 KINGS RD, CHELSEA
TEL: 351 - 0764. P.M.

OR FROM BOX OFFICE
SCREEN ON THE GREEN (ISLINGTON GREEN)

Sex Pistols

GROUPS
VED BY

What more could a young band want?

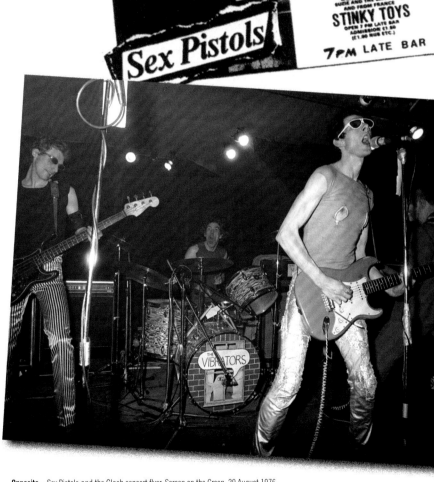

ANARCHY IN THE U.K.

PUNK special
100 CLUB
100 OXFORD ST.
Monday SEPTEMBER 20
SEX PISTOLS
CLASH
SUB WAY SECT
SIOUX AND THE BANSHEES
AND FROM FRANCE
STINKY TOYS
OPEN 7 PM LATE BAR
ADMISSION £1.50
(£1.00 SUB ETC.)
7PM LATE BAR

Sex Pistols

THE VIBRATORS

Plenty of people were dismissing their music as tuneless rubbish. But the Pistols were being taken very seriously in quarters that mattered. A sense of a rapidly spreading youthful uprising was emboldened by an event at the Screen on the Green in Islington on 31 August, featuring the Sex Pistols, the Clash and Buzzcocks. Three weeks later, on 20 and 21 September, an even bigger event at the 100 Club saw those bands joined by the Damned, Siouxsie and the Banshees (with Sid Vicious on drums), the Vibrators, Vic Godard's Subway Sect and French punk band Stinky Toys. It was a major gathering of the clans, while the audience included Paul Weller, Chrissie Hynde, Shane MacGowan and members of the Adverts.

Meanwhile, the Pistols had also been recording, laying down "Pretty Vacant", "Problems" and "No Feelings" on 15 May at the 24-track Majestic Studios in London, a former cinema. Their producer Chris Spedding, was a renowned guitarist who'd had a hit in 1975 with "Motor Bikin'". The session – which Matlock claims was paid for by RAK Records' glam rock impresario Mickie Most – captures the band in their raw, untamed and effervescent early state, with scant studio gloss.

Opposite – Sex Pistols and the Clash concert flyer, Screen on the Green, 29 August 1976.

Top – "Anarchy in the U.K." tour poster, 100 Club, London, 20 September 1976.

Bottom – The Vibrators, the Nashville, London, 29 April 1977.

"Two guitar overdubs, that was about it,"
Spedding told *Anarchy in the Year Zero* author
Clinton Heylin. "I asked them to do a rehearsal
for me and I switched on the [tape] recorder. So
they thought they were doing a rehearsal and they
were actually doing their first take." For all the
paper talk of being into chaos, not music,
Spedding was impressed by how well the four-
some played together and their musicality. "I
found it very weird, all that in the press about
them not playing music," he said. "If they were
notable for one thing it was that. They were
always in time and in tune. I couldn't understand
why some had chosen to attack them. They've got
cloth ears."

The group were less enthusiastic about the
recordings. In *Anger is an Energy*, Rotten
describes a "fantastic" session which had

"showed us the possibilities of the studio," but
Jones found it "bland and drab," preferring a
second session in July 1976, where Dave
Goodman had recorded them playing in the
rehearsal room. The Pistols' trusty sound man's
four-track recording (overdubs subsequently
added on an eight-track) contained "Anarchy in
the U.K.", "Pretty Vacant", "Seventeen",
"Satellite", "Problems", "I Wanna Be Me" and
"Submission". Although raw and rough this
collection was almost a prototype for an album.
With these recordings and a bulging press pack,
McLaren approached major labels … to negative
response.

Violence had crept into the punk scene, which
certainly didn't help matters. Sid Vicious had
attacked *NME*'s Nick Kent with a bike chain (an
incident which saw the publication show less

Mercer, who presumably didn't like being thought of as a dinosaur, duly relented. On 8 October, the Sex Pistols signed a £40,000 two-year deal with the label that had brought the world the Beatles, celebrating the occasion with champagne, which Jones subsequently spewed up in the parking lot. The next day, the revelation that – horror of horrors – the Sex Pistols had vomited at their record company's premises was all over the papers, which was a glimpse of controversies to come. However, in the Pistols camp, a far more pressing issue was that the Damned had also signed a deal, and it was them, not the Pistols, who released British punk's first record.

"New Rose", released on Stiff Records on 22 October 1976, was, and is, a classic. It was produced by Nick Lowe in a tiny eight-track studio that was perfect for the Damned's early raw, amphetamine warrior charge. "We spent more time in the pub round the corner than we spent recording, but Nick captured how wild we sounded," guitarist/songwriter Brian James told me in a *Guardian* interview in 2018. "We thought we were a fast rock 'n' roll band, but after Caroline Coon had coined the term 'punk rock' suddenly New Rose was 'the first British punk single'. Everything happened very quickly after that."

Meanwhile, the Sex Pistols' own punk classic debut, "Anarchy in the U.K.", was recorded

support for the Pistols for a while, owing to his association with the band). Furthermore, Vicious served time in Ashford Remand Centre after a hurled glass at the 100 Club festival left a girl with serious eye injuries. Still, when Polydor's Chris Parry played the Goodman tapes for his bosses, it was the music that left them unimpressed, not the bad reputations associated with their brand of punk.

EMI were similarly unenthusiastic. "It sounded fucking awful to me," general manager Bob Mercer reflected later. "I said, 'No way'." However, when Mercer returned to the EMI offices he was besieged by the A&R department, who argued that the Pistols might not be slick or radio-friendly, but they were what was happening on the street. "What do you know?" he was told. "You're over 30!"

IT SOUNDED FUCKING AWFUL TO ME. I SAID, 'NO WAY'.

Bob Mercer, EMI

twice. They recorded the first version (with Dave Goodman) for Polydor, before the label threw the band out of the studio when they realised that they'd signed to EMI. However, EMI rejected the Goodman recording, so days later, they were back in the studio again. This time, Roxy Music producer Chris Thomas was at the controls in London's Wessex studios, with Bill Price engineering. With Queen recording next door, the now famous version of "Anarchy …" was recorded. Price remembers as many as 19 or 20 takes, but according to Matlock most of the released song was from take three, with the second part from take five. More guitars were then "built up". Thomas – Roxy fan Cook's suggestion as producer – later recalled how Johnny Rotten had arrived in a bad mood, aiming sullen barbs at the producer, perceiving him to be an emissary of the rock establishment. But John Lydon was soon as committed as any of them to "making a great record".

In a 2018 interview for *The Guardian*, the singer told me that his instantly recognisable laugh which begins the song had been spontaneous. "I suddenly had a microphone and the realisation that words can be very powerful and

thrilling. I was thinking: 'Ah-ha! Look what I've got a chance to do.'"

The song was released in a plain black sleeve on 28 November, backed with "I Wanna Be Me", and promoted by features in the major music papers. *Melody Maker*'s Caroline Coon found Rotten already relishing the role of provocateur and quote machine. "Everyone is so fed up with the old way," he explained. "We are constantly being dictated to by musical old farts out of university who've got rich parents." He added: "If the single gets into the chart then it will show that it's all been worth it – that there are thousands of people who are pissed off with everything."

For *NME*'s Julie Burchill and Tony Parsons, the newly recruited "hip young gunslingers" hired specifically to cover new music, "Anarchy in the U.K." was "the greatest youth frustration anthem ever released. Just over three minutes of blind raging fury." *Sniffin' Glue* fanzine's influential Mark Perry claimed that the song "destroys all the rock 'n' roll laws. Just by getting this thing released the Pistols have kicked the establishment right in the balls … it is the most important record that's ever been released."

Above – Johnny Rotten in 1976.
Opposite – *Sniffin' Glue*, July 1977.

SNIFFIN' GLUE
AND OTHER SELF-DEFENCE HABITS...
JULY '77

30p

SO TELL US....
WHAT D'YA THINK ISSUE NUMBER 11

"IT IS THE MOST _IMPORTANT_ RECORD THAT'S EVER BEEN RELEASED.
SNIFFIN' GLUE **"**

"**THE GREATEST YOUTH FRUSTRATION ANTHEM EVER RELEASED. JUST OVER THREE MINUTES OF <u>BLIND RAGING FURY</u>.**

N.ME ""

The single premiered on the BBC's popular mainstream news programme *Nationwide*, before that fateful appearance on Bill Grundy's show changed everything overnight. After that, life in and around the Pistols would never be the same again. The morning after *Today*, on 2 December, there was panic at EMI, while a hastily arranged interview with Radio Luxembourg (set up to get the band out of the country and away from the descending media) contained so many bleeped out swear words it sounded like Morse code. Then the first show of the "Anarchy Tour" (featuring the Pistols, the Clash, the Damned and the Heartbreakers over 19 nights) at the University of East Anglia was suddenly cancelled. This was because the university's Vice Chancellor, Dr Frank Thistlethwaite, pulled the gig "on the grounds of protecting the safety and security of persons and property."

By now, the band were at the forefront of a full-on moral panic. In Derby, councillors tried to get all the bands to "audition" to decide whether to let them play. According to the Damned's bassist Captain Sensible, their tour manager had agreed to this, without telling the band. McLaren regarded this as so disloyal he threw them off the tour, by which time dates were tumbling like dominoes. With more tabloid fury by the day, EMI's record packers went on strike because

they'd refused to handle the single, which was hurriedly withdrawn and deleted after charting at No. 38. In all, 13 of the "Anarchy Tour"'s projected 19 shows were cancelled.

In *Lonely Boy*, Jones argues that the outing "should have been one of the highlights of the whole punk thing – us at the peak of our powers on a nationwide tour with the Clash, the Damned and Johnny Thunders and the Heartbreakers, who Malcolm had flown over from New York to give us an American angle. I think they arrived on the night after the Grundy thing, so they didn't know what kind of shitstorm they were walking into. Everyone was fucking banning us. It was exciting at first … But it got boring pretty quickly." Thus, the cream of British punk rock ended up travelling the country in a huge bus, unsure whether venues or hotels would have them.

The first show that did take place was at Leeds Polytechnic on 6 December, although the *Melody Maker*'s Caroline Coon was less enthusiastic than she had been previously. Reporting how Rotten had been greeted by the audience like a victorious trooper, and had dedicated the event to "local councillors, Bill Grundy and the Queen," she noted how otherwise it took "'Johnny' a whole set to allay the audience's suspicion of him." The following morning,

Opposite – Rotten onstage at Leeds Polytechnic during the "Anarchy Tour", 6 December 1976.

Below – The Heartbreakers at CBGB, including future Voidoids singer Richard Hell.

the *Daily Mirror* front page reported acts of vandalism at the city's Dragonara hotel. Of how, egged on by reporters, the band had "hurled plant pots around the lobby and scattered soil over the carpets. As they walked away, they shouted 'Don't blame us. It's what you wanted. Send the bill to EMI.'" As Matlock later admitted in his book, the media and their own management were casting the Pistols in roles they were happy to play: "Snottiness had become a big part of being a Sex Pistol. We all got a taste for it, as it became expected of us."

Meanwhile, manager McLaren cheerily informed the *Daily Mirror* that the high spot of the gigs would be "a song that opens with the words, *'God bless the Queen, and her fascist regime.'*" This latest arrival in the setlist was initially called "No Future". Meanwhile, as the press asked members of the public for their views on "the punk shockers", rock 'n' roller Bill Haley – whose own concerts in the 1950s had seen rockers tearing up the seats – told the media that these outrageous punk rockers' bad language was "carrying things too far."

By the time the tour reached Manchester's Electric Circus, a representative from the increasingly panicked record label had been sent to give the group a good old-fashioned British talking to, after they were being routinely turfed out of hotels and tailed by the police. After the Cardiff gig was cancelled, the Castle Cinema in Caerphilly emerged as an alternative venue, despite letters in the *South Wales Echo* protesting against the cinema management's decision to engage a "'punk rock group' already notorious for its dependence on obscenity, blasphemy and open violence."

As nearby shops and amenities closed for 24 hours around the concert, the show was picketed by a Christian choir and a Pentecostal preacher, who were averse to the "*anti-Christ*" line in "Anarchy" and told the somewhat bemused band they were "the Devil's children." Leaflets were distributed in Caerphilly town centre, claiming trends such as punk were "clearly part of the fulfilment of Jesus' prophecy that before his return to earth, wickedness would multiply beyond all previous limits." The wickedness – sorry, gig – did take place, on 14 December, before an audience including subsequent New Romantic/Visage founder Steve Strange, who later claimed to have been the first punk in Wales.

Afterwards, Rotten told local rock fanzine *Penarth's Buzz* of his surprise that "many grown-up adults can behave so ludicrously childishly. Don't they know their papers tell them lies? I don't think they do – they live in a twilight zone.

"EVERYONE WAS FUCKING BANNING US. IT WAS EXCITING AT FIRST ... BUT IT GOT BORING PRETTY QUICKLY.

Jones

That's alright, they can be happy in their own way, but I don't think they've got the right to interrupt my way; each to their own, God loves all kinds."

Meanwhile, Bernard Brook-Partridge, the Conservative Chairman of the Arts Committee of the Greater London Council, raged on television that punk was: "nauseating, disgusting, degrading, ghastly, sleazy, prurient, voyeuristic … I think that most of these groups would be improved by sudden death. The worst of the punk rock groups are the Sex Pistols. They are unbelievably nauseating, the antithesis of humankind. I would like to see somebody dig a very, very large exceedingly deep hole and drop the whole bloody lot down it. You know, I think

the whole world would be vastly improved by their total and utter non-existence."

Years later, in *Anger is an Energy*, Rotten correctly argued that the band had been "an easy target, a bunch of saucy boys from the wrong side of town who were making a racket and were easy to shoot down." By then, Caerphilly councillor Ray Davies – who had led the town's resistance in 1976 – seemed to have come round to a similar view. Speaking to BBC South Wales in 2006, he told of his "great regrets when I look back at it because who am I, a fuddy-duddy councillor, to tell young people what they should listen to, what they should enjoy and how they should conduct themselves and their lives?"

Pages 84–85 – Anarchy in (checks notes) Yorkshire. The Sex Pistols onstage at Leeds Polytechnic, 6 December 1976.

Above – The Sex Pistols play at the Castle Cinema in Caerphilly, Wales as part of the "Anarchy Tour", 14 December 1976.

"YOU KNOW, I THINK THE WHOLE WORLD WOULD BE VASTLY IMPROVED BY THEIR TOTAL AND UTTER NON-EXISTENCE.

Bernard Brook-Partridge

After shows in Liverpool, Cardiff and Guildford were also cancelled, the band returned to the Electric Circus in Manchester for a repeat performance (on the 19th), although this time fans including Joy Division's Peter Hook were greeted with a hail of bottles and objects from the flats above. After a Torquay gig was pulled, the beleaguered tour limped into Plymouth for two nights at the Woods Centre which Matlock rated the best of the whole tour – not that there was much competition, with only six shows played.

"We were so happy that it was all over," he told *Mojo* in 2000. "We didn't even bother to change into our stage clothes, just played for each other. Each band got up and played and then handed their instruments to the next band." At least EMI sent them a Christmas present – a hamper full of food, which arrived on Christmas Eve. In 2000, Caroline Coon told *Mojo* how she cooked Christmas dinner for the Pistols, the Damned and the Clash the next day, at a house rented by *Sounds* writer/Pistols fan Jonh Ingham. "Then the Heartbreakers turned up and the mood changed horribly. They were so rude and nasty, showing the English kids how to shoot up heroin."

In early interviews, McLaren had always claimed the Pistols didn't take drugs – such behaviour was seen as old hat and establishment – although in reality amphetamine sulphate – "speed" – had become the drug of choice. It suited the music – hard and fast – and was cheap, not expensive or associated with the rock aristocracy like cocaine, or extended psychedelic jams about fish, caused by LSD.

However, the Heartbreakers brought heroin into the heart of the scene. The band's drummer, Jerry Nolan, formerly of the New York Dolls, even "shot up" Rotten with the class A drug, an incident both came to regret. "I thought 'I want to know what the big taboo is'," Rotten reflects in *Anger is an Energy*. "I can't be preaching against it unless I've sampled the goods." It made him sick and he never touched the stuff again, deciding that users were "running away from creativity" and making themselves "pointless."

Coon eventually asked the Heartbreakers to leave the premises, but Rotten's pal Sid Vicious would experience a more enduring and ultimately fatal dalliance with the drug. The shocking manner of Vicious's demise was just one of many storms to come.

Pages 88–89 – 1977, just before Sid Vicious joined the band.

Opposite top – The Heartbreakers. L–R: Walter Lure, Jerry Nolan, Richard Hell, Johnny Thunders.

Opposite bottom – "Drinks are on me": Rotten hands a can of beer to fans while onstage at Leeds Polytechnic during their "Anarchy Tour" gig, 6 December 1976.

FROM SEX PISTOL to EX PISTOL

In late 1976, McLaren's in-house Pistols fanzine declared: "There is but one criteria, does it threaten the status quo?" By the start of 1977, with the Grundy appearance still rumbling on in the tabloids, a number of people felt the Sex Pistols were indeed threatening the established order. Certainly, punk had become a focus for all sorts of complaints about youth in general and an easy scapegoat for anything considered anti-establishment or anti-social. Tabloid hysteria had led to more moral panic, as authority figures and disgruntled members of the public lined up in the press to shoot the band down. Some of the pot-shots were landing very close to home.

Conservative Member of Parliament for Christchurch Robert Adley wrote to EMI, accusing the self-styled "Greatest Recording Organisation in the World" of "financing a bunch of ill-mannered louts who seem to cause offence wherever they go." Adley urged chairman Sir John Read to drop the band, insisting, "Surely a group of your size and reputation could forgo the doubtful privilege of sponsoring trash like the Sex Pistols."

More worryingly for the band, Read seemed to share such sentiments, declaring, "[the Pistols'] style of attack on our society is something I greatly resent." Meanwhile, another EMI director, former Attorney General Lord Shawcross, told the *Daily Express* he felt the company were being "taken for a ride."

Unease in the label's higher echelons was spreading down the ranks. A&R man John Bagnall – who'd previously shown allegiance by ditching his old flares and turning up to work with safety pins in tighter trousers – had quietly resumed wearing his pre-punk clobber. The fact that the Pistols were on EMI at all felt incongruous.

Below – Steve Jones, Johnny Rotten, Glen Matlock and Paul Cook.

> ## "WE WANTED PUBLICITY FOR THEM, BUT NOT OF <u>THAT</u> KIND AND NOT OF THAT MAGNITUDE."
> ### Leslie Hill, EMI

This was the label of the Beatles, Pink Floyd, Cliff Richard and (er) cider-drinking country types the Wurzels (a comic folk band). EMI was the epitome of corporate middle England, who manufactured defence systems and brain scanners as well as pop records. Matlock felt like the band had "signed to the BBC," much later telling *Sex Pistols: 90 Days at EMI* author Brian Southall that for him the growing schism between band and label was a microcosm of a wider trend: "establishment vs anti-establishment."

Speculation grew that, with the ink on the Pistols' contract barely dry, the company might tear it up. Chairman Read said as much to the company's annual general meeting, to which McLaren was quoted in the *Daily Mail* responding, "Tell him to go fuck himself." Once again, in order to take the heat off the band, the manager took them to Holland to play two gigs in Amsterdam. However, they'd got no further than Heathrow airport before it all kicked off again.

"Revolting!" raged the front page headline of the *Evening News* on 4 January, the text below claiming, "The Sex Pistols shocked and revolted passengers and airline staff as they vomited and spat their way to an Amsterdam flight." An unnamed and thus unverifiable airline ticket desk attendant was quoted as saying, "The group are the most revolting people I have ever seen in my life. They were disgusting, sick and obscene. The group called us filthy names and insulted

everyone in sight." A traveller, Mrs Freda van Roiden from Rotterdam, was also quoted, declaring, wonderfully, "I think they had been drinking and they looked as if they needed a good wash."

Over a year later, EMI Managing Director Leslie Hill insisted in *Sex Pistols: The Inside Story* that the "so-called vomiting and spitting" never actually took place. "We had a man with them every minute of the day and that never happened." Hill denied the band had ever been near the ticket desk, never mind behaved obscenely. "They didn't go to the ticket desk because they were late for the plane. Our guy went and got the tickets for them." Nevertheless, the damage was done, and Hill was fed up having to spend half his working days fielding controversies about the Pistols.

"We hoped the [bad publicity] would blow over and the group themselves would be less provocative," he told interviewer Judy Vermorel. "We couldn't promote the records in that situation. We wanted publicity for them, but not of that kind and not of that magnitude."

On 6 January, EMI buckled. With McLaren still in Amsterdam, Hill announced that after intense discussion he and McLaren had agreed to terminate the contract, but then suggested the manager "chose to change his mind." McLaren denied there had been a "mutual termination" or indeed any termination at all. "That's rubbish," he told the BBC. "I haven't signed a single paper. As

Above – "Bit of a lunatic. A front-man who had definite ideas": Johnny Rotten (John Lydon) performing live onstage, Notre Dame Hall, London, 15 November 1976.

far as I'm concerned, we're still on EMI." Meanwhile, an EMI statement insisted: "EMI feels it is unable to promote this group's records internationally in view of the adverse publicity generated over the past two months, although recent press reports of the group's behaviour appear to have been exaggerated." Establishment and anti-establishment had indeed collided.

Guitarist Jones later argued that "the boss of EMI used to have tea with the Queen" and "didn't want to be associated with these foul mouthed yobs anymore." Whatever the truth of that one, for Rotten it was simply a mismatch of minds. "I suppose EMI thought it would be a giggle fest and they really couldn't cope with what it actually was," he reflects in *Anger is an Energy.* "The hardcore edge just rocked them onto their foundations, so it was just get out of EMI quick."

With the hastily withdrawn "Anarchy in the U.K." already a collector's item, the band departed the label with the remainder of the £40,000 and the inspiration for *Never Mind the Bollocks* highlight "EMI (Unlimited Supply)". The Pistols' two-year contract had lasted 90 days. Meanwhile, there was another burning issue,

Opposite – Glen Matlock.

described in McLaren's PA Sophie Richmond's diary of 20 January 1977 as "the continuing problem of Glen."

The Pistols weren't totally dysfunctional but had never been best buddies. Cook and Jones were tight, having been childhood friends, but Matlock had never been one of the gang, and while Rotten and Jones got on well enough, the singer was a perennial outsider and cracks widened once he became the focus of the press attention. Matlock felt that publicity had inflated Rotten's ego, while the singer argued the opposite, telling *Inside Story* authors the Vermorels that "Glen was an ego tripper, a very bad one."

In *Lonely Boy*, Jones argues that, onstage at least, such tensions between band members was part of what drew people in. "It's not like I was giving Johnny dirty looks all the time while he was winding the crowd up or blowing his nose or whatever he was doing. It's just that's what the source of the energy is. Sometimes people would get the wrong end of the stick when it came to the flare ups we'd have onstage."

Such tension in their performances was one thing, but being prevented from gigging had

GLEN WAS AN EGO TRIPPER, A VERY BAD ONE.

Rotten

"WE BECAME FRUSTRATED AND BEGAN LOOKING AT EACH OTHER SUSPICIOUSLY."

Matlock

Below – Sex Pistols at EMI press conference, December 1976. EMI ended the contract with the group in January 1977 because of their behaviour in public.

Opposite – Sex Pistols at Paradiso, Amsterdam, 6 January 1977.

started to turn the Pistols more seriously and personally against each other. "We became frustrated and began looking at each other suspiciously," Rotten admits in *Rotten: The Autobiography.* "We were bored and at each other's backs."

Matlock and Rotten had become particularly estranged. Having rowed during the writing of "Submission", tensions flared again during a gig at the 100 Club where Rotten sang different lyrics to the song that was being played. After he left the stage and was subsequently found outside, McLaren reportedly told him to apologise or be turfed out of the group. Matlock has since told how the singer would reject his ideas for songs with comments such as "Why don't you drop dead?" The bassist has also suggested that Rotten wasn't happy with him hanging out with the Clash's Mick Jones on the "Anarchy Tour", while Steve Jones has said that the Pistols felt that Matlock had become too close to EMI (who had certainly offered him a solo deal).

Whatever the ins and outs of it, Glen Matlock, bassist and songwriter, was behind some of their best songs. And he wasn't prepared to be a yes man and would defend his point of view. Matlock has told a story alleging that Rotten once turned up to rehearsals with a hammer, wanting a showdown. This was not quite the behaviour you'd expect during rehearsals, and it prompted Matlock to walk out. Similarly to Jones, Matlock had admitted the tensions fuelled the music, although the guitarist tends to cite the example of the Who – whose infamous in-fighting ranged

from singer Roger Daltrey lamping guitarist Pete Townshend, to drummer Keith Moon also turning up to rehearsals with an axe. He marvelled at how the Who stayed together where the Pistols were doomed to fail.

With hindsight, both bassist and singer have suspected that they were being played off against each other and perhaps they were. "The things I was led to believe about Glen, and I'm sure Glen was led to believe things about me," Rotten reflects in *Rotten: The Autobiography*. "Somebody told us a crock of shit and it was nasty, evil, spiteful, vindictive and manipulative." Matlock noticed things starting to change after September 1976, when McLaren's company Glitterbest got them to sign a management contract taking 25 per cent of the band's income plus his expenses. Fundamentally, as he told *Sex Pistols: The Inside Story,* "It was getting out of our hands a bit. Malcolm had taken even more control." Quietly and subtly, what would become a full-blown war between McLaren and Rotten had escalated some more.

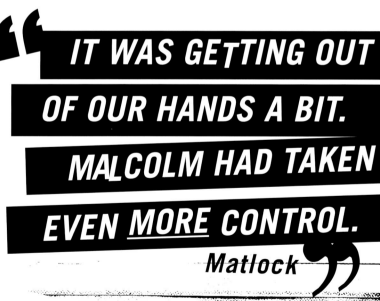

> **"IT WAS GETTING OUT OF OUR HANDS A BIT. MALCOLM HAD TAKEN EVEN MORE CONTROL.**
> **— Matlock"**

Opposite – Sex Pistols perform at Paradiso, Amsterdam.

Above – Malcolm McLaren and (behind) Steve Jones, 10 March 1977.

Pages 102–103 — Glen Matlock, Johnny Rotten (aka John Lydon), Steve Jones and Paul Cook.

Above — Sex Pistols at Paradiso.

 FOR ALL THE BIG CONTRIBUTIONS HE MADE TO THE SONGWRITING AND GETTING THE BAND OFF THE GROUND, HE JUST DIDN'T FIT INTO THE URCHIN VIBE.

Jones

Matlock was foremost in asking awkward questions about where the money was going, as Jones has since described. He asserts that the manager "certainly knew how to stir the shit-pot," writing in *Lonely Boy* how he "couldn't really put my finger on the exact nature of those manipulations, but they were definitely going on."

Slowly, Matlock had felt ostracised and now began to distance himself. By early 1977, he'd stopped wearing the clothes from SEX (now renamed Seditionaries) and his hair was neater. His Pistols days were numbered.

"For all the big contributions he made to the songwriting and getting the band off the ground, he just didn't fit into the urchin vibe," Jones admits in *Lonely Boy.* "Rotten calling him a 'mummy's boy' was unfair, but Matlock never quite looked the part. You could see he'd never gone without a meal, and he'd started to act up to being the toff of the group in a way that was quite embarrassing."

For Cook's part, he told *Sex Pistols: The Inside Story* that "Everyone got on alright for ages, then Glen just started going in a different direction. You know, his parents and that were different … and he went to grammar school and that, and art school. He was sort of different anyway. Right from the beginning."

Months, if not years, of tensions came to a head in Amsterdam, where Matlock, still only 19, also received the news of the parting from EMI. Relations with Rotten were as bad as ever. He'd basically had enough. After a second show at the Paradiso club he refused to perform an encore. "I was just fed up being in the same place as John," he writes in *I Was a Teenage Sex Pistol*. "He was totally conceited, arrogant and stroppy, just for the sake of it … I flew back to London and that was it."

Whatever McLaren's machinations, the parting of the ways had come down to an old-fashioned personality clash. At a band management meeting – without Rotten – Matlock admitted he couldn't

stand the singer. One of them had to go, and it couldn't be the frontman. Everything seemed set up for an amicable parting of the ways, but then McLaren put out an absurd but image-friendly statement saying the bassist had been sacked "for liking the Beatles."

Matlock did indeed care for the Fab Four, but this was hardly the reason for his departure. In one fell swoop, the Pistols lost a key member, a bassist and the person who'd written the music for "Anarchy in the U.K.", "God Save the Queen" and the music and most of the words of "Pretty Vacant" – arguably the top three Pistols classics. That sort of input couldn't easily be replaced – and Jones, for one, has since admitted it was a mistake to lose him. Still, there would shortly be another record company … and another bass player.

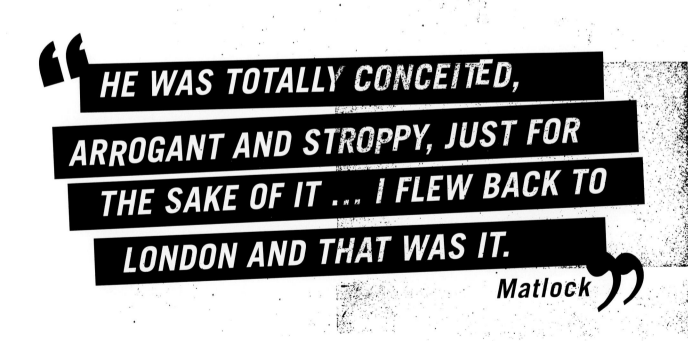

"HE WAS TOTALLY CONCEITED, ARROGANT AND STROPPY, JUST FOR THE SAKE OF IT … I FLEW BACK TO LONDON AND THAT WAS IT.

Matlock

APPETITE FOR DESTRUCTION (AND VODKA)

Helpfully, Matlock's replacement was close at hand. Sid Vicious was the same age (19), had a striking, spiky-haired punk image and had been there or thereabouts from the beginning. In October 1976, he'd been quoted in a Jonh Ingham *Sounds* article about punk, expressing appropriately nihilistic sentiments ("I've only ever been in love with a beer bottle and a mirror"). According to Rotten, Vicious had even invented the pogo, the punk dance which resembled a leaping centre forward scoring a header. Their close friendship would also (in theory at least) mean the singer would finally have an ally in the band.

On the other hand, Vicious couldn't play the instrument or write songs and had a *reputation*. Friends remember him as sweet, sharp, sensitive, intelligent and funny, but he was suggestible, with a troubling psychotic side evinced by the incidents with rock journalist Nick Kent and at the 100 Club. Nevertheless, rumours that Vicious would indeed replace Matlock surfaced as early as 20 February 1977, although these were swiftly denied by McLaren's PA, Sophie Richmond.

Vicious had been born John Simon Ritchie in London on 10 May 1957, and brought up by his mother. Anne Beverley, whose surname he later adopted, had had a hard life. She was abandoned by her unmarried mother aged 12, married young (her second husband died of kidney failure just six months later) and had her child with another man, a trombonist, who didn't stick around to watch him grow. Being brought up without a father figure in numerous homes (in Tunbridge Wells, Bristol and Stoke Newington), he wasn't really "vicious" in his youth but certainly knew how to look after himself. Beverley and Lydon (Rotten) both attended Kingsway Princeton College of Further Education. Actor Timothy Spall told *The Guardian* in 2021 how he'd been buying a bacon sandwich in the refectory when he encountered "this very peculiar guy in a black leather jacket, very tight trousers, very white face, spiky hair, looking down on everybody eating with a look of Shakespearean, malevolent disdain. That was Sid Vicious."

Below – John Simon Ritchie (1957–1979) aka Sid Vicous, Sex Pistol, when he was a young boy aged 12, 1969.

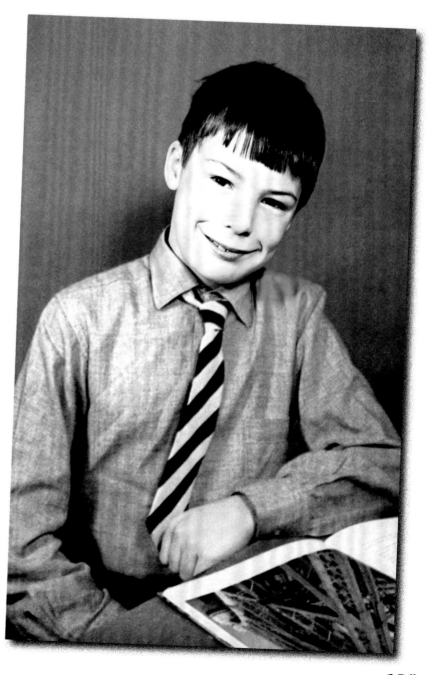

John Lydon suggested the name (after a pet hamster) and he also gave his new friend the famous spiky haircut. Sid Vicious was a David Bowie fan, who wasn't averse to a bit of Abba. He was often homeless and drifted between squats before the pair ended up sharing a place in Hampstead after Lydon was also turfed out by his parents. Lydon occasionally worked in Crank's restaurant; Vicious briefly worked in a clothing factory before scratching a living selling "speed". Jah Wobble, another friend, who made the sensitively handled and illuminating 2009 radio documentary *In Search of Sid*, remembers him as "a very damaged boy."

England's Dreaming author Jon Savage allowed access to his recordings of Vicious's mother for this radio documentary. In 2015, Wobble told me, "She was a heroin addict – going, 'I fucking told him, I don't care where you go. Sling yer hook. Fuck off. Sleep on a park bench for all I care.' This when Sid was 15 years of age. When Sid told a shrink that he wanted to kill himself, the shrink told him to bring a friend along to get him interested in life, and that was me. I said, 'To be honest, I don't know if he has got anything worth living for. Suicide is a viable option.' The shrink was horrified – we ran out of there pissing ourselves laughing. But, of course, many a true word said in jest. He really did want to top himself." Other friends were shocked when, aged 18, Vicious killed a cat for kicks, an incident he'd later reference in his hit version of "My Way".

Opposite – Too fast to live, too young to die: Sid Vicious of the Sex Pistols in Holland, December 1977.

Top – Jah Wobble performing onstage.

Bottom – Sid Vicious, doing it "My Way".

Above – Sid Vicious with Nancy Spungen outside Marylebone Magistrates' Court, where they faced drugs charges.

Opposite – Sid Vicious injects himself with heroin in 1978. Within a year, he was dead from a drugs overdose, after being charged with killing his girlfriend, Nancy Spungen, in a New York hotel.

Leaving such darkly disturbing tendencies aside, Vicious was a great, mischievous wag (who once famously said "I've met the man in the street and he's a c***") and shared his pals' caustic wit and sense of humour. Asked what he brought to the Sex Pistols, the new bassist described the new-look line-up as "much more handsome." Well … Vicious certainly looked inimitably punk and truly iconic. His leather jacket, raven black spiky hair and *Vive le Rock* T-shirt soon became a regular sighting on the British high street. Having been the Banshees' drummer for that one ramshackle gig and fronted the short-lived Flowers of Romance, who played no gigs at all, more than anything Vicious yearned to be in a group. Once Rotten joined them, he particularly coveted a place in the Pistols. Meanwhile, for McLaren, Vicious offered a ready-made source of outrage, only much more than he planned for.

Shortly after becoming a Sex Pistol, Vicious acquired Nancy Spungen as a girlfriend, which was another connection that would come to define his life and death. The 19-year-old Nancy was a year younger, much more worldly and far more emotionally disturbed than he was. Her appetite for destruction and particularly self-destruction is summed up by the title of her own mother's book about her, *And I Do Not Want to Live This Life*. Born in Philadelphia, after a traumatic delivery, Spungen had been so hyperactive as a child that she was first taken for therapy aged just three. She'd been placed in intensive psychiatric therapy aged just 11, the age she first expressed a wish to die. Aged 17, after running away to New York, she had briefly taken up with Richard Hell before becoming notorious on the Big Apple scene as a go-getter and junkie who funded her habit with prostitution. When she

arrived in London in early 1977, she'd unsuccessfully tried to hook up with Rotten, but Vicious proved more encouraging.

Indeed, the pair became inseparable and loved each other, although theirs was a dark, twisted, loving but nihilistic mutual adoration. Vicious was no stranger to hard drug use. In 2007, writing in *The Independent On Sunday*, Wobble recalled his shock, as a 16-year-old, of seeing Vicious injecting drugs with his mother. But it was Spungen who introduced the Pistol to intravenous heroin, which distanced him from several longstanding friends. Vicious was cast into his final, fatal role, of leather-jacketed bringer of what McLaren called "attitude" but this would include chaos, disaster and untimely death.

In *England's Dreaming*, Heartbreakers manager Leee Black Childers describes how a "cold chill ran down my spine once I heard that Sid had hooked up with Nancy. And from that day on, Sid was no longer the person that I knew."

"[A] COLD CHILL RAN DOWN MY SPINE ONCE I HEARD THAT SID HAD HOOKED UP WITH NANCY. AND FROM THAT DAY ON, SID WAS NO LONGER THE PERSON THAT I KNEW."

Leee Black Childers

Similarly, Rotten has described how heroin turned his friend into a "zombie", while in *Lonely Boy*, Jones observes how the bassist felt he had to act "a certain way" once he'd been christened Vicious. "From the minute Sid joined the band, nothing was ever normal again," he writes. "I hadn't minded being second fiddle to John, but now I was playing third fiddle to a fucking idiot. Fourth if you went along with Malcolm's increasingly delusional certainty that we were all his puppets." Jones has come to regret his much-repeated quote about the Pistols not being about music, but chaos. "Be careful what you fucking wish for. Now we'd got chaos, and it was shit."

> " **FROM THE MINUTE SID JOINED THE BAND, NOTHING WAS EVER NORMAL AGAIN. I HADN'T MINDED BEING SECOND FIDDLE TO JOHN, BUT NOW I WAS PLAYING THIRD FIDDLE TO A FUCKING IDIOT.** "
>
> Jones

Right — The Sex Pistols in the Netherlands.

The first change was that Jones had to play bass on the Pistols' recordings, because Vicious wasn't up to it. He didn't mind so much, but was less keen on having to painstakingly try to teach Vicious how to play the bass runs live. Motorhead bassist/singer Lemmy also had a go at teaching him to play, but Vicious never got the hang of it and at some gigs the band didn't bother to plug him in. Sometimes, he'd play the one bass line that he could play, over and over again, no matter which song was being played. At other times he'd just stand there, looking the part but mainly operating as provocateur. That may have been why McLaren chose him, but the manager had no idea what he was letting them all in for. He'd encountered heroin with the New York Dolls – and been unprepared to cope with it then. With Vicious, he didn't even know about the problem until it was too late.

As author Fred Vermorel reflects in *1977: The Bollocks Diaries*, "The interview Sid did with [Vermorel's then wife] Judy for *Sex Pistols: The Inside Story* was the only in-depth one he did. When I transcribed the tape I realised he was seriously ill. He wasn't doing it for laughs. Putting him in a band like that when he's on heroin is a recipe for disaster."

Equally, the new arrival was not popular in the camp. McLaren's PA, Sophie Richmond, found him "immature". Even Rotten stopped being a close friend after Sid took up with Spungen. By February 1977, the Pistols had released one single, the hastily deleted "Anarchy in the U.K.", played just two gigs that year (Matlock's last, in Amsterdam), lost a record contract and their best tunesmith, and recruited a bass player that couldn't play. Meanwhile, others were catching up, and punk was no longer such a cult.

The Roxy club in Covent Garden was proving a popular showcase for the prime movers (other than the Pistols, who never played there). Drainpipes (very tight trousers) were starting to be glimpsed amidst the flares and bell bottoms on the high street. Hair was shorter and spikier and there was a blossoming subculture of fanzines, T-shirts and badges. Meanwhile, the major labels were snapping up the groups. Polydor signed the Jam and Siouxsie and the Banshees; CBS took on the Clash. Wire signed to EMI/Harvest (Pink Floyd's imprint). The Damned released a second single, "Neat Neat Neat", on Stiff.

Left – Sid with girlfriend Nancy Spungen and Lemmy from Motorhead.

Meanwhile, up in Manchester, Buzzcocks had come a long way since that Pistols support slot at the Lesser Free Trade Hall, having been catapulted to national attention by reviews of that self-same show. Once the record labels started snapping up London punk bands, Buzzcocks realised they had to make their mark or risk being passed by. However, A&R scouts didn't venture up to Manchester.

"The place felt like the tide had gone out," manager Richard Boon told me for a *Guardian* article in 2017. There were a handful of London-based independent labels, but to guitarist Pete Shelley, the idea of manufacturing a record themselves felt "as unfeasible as making a computer in your front room." However, that's exactly what they did.

Four songs, including the classic "Boredom", were produced by Martin "Zero" Hannett (now more famous as the producer behind Joy Division and early New Order). Buzzcocks borrowed £500 to press up 1000 copies and spent all night putting them into the sleeves, which were

illustrated by a band shot taken by Boon with a hand-held Polaroid camera. Once record shops in Manchester and London took the single, they began selling like hot cakes. The *Spiral Scratch* EP ended up selling 16,000 copies and making the Top 40.

Singer Howard Devoto's idea of providing recording details on the sleeve – "'Breakdown', 3rd take No dubs" and so on – further demystified the process of making records, making it seem accessible to scores of young groups. Two months after *Spiral Scratch* was released, the Desperate Bicycles formed, and released a single with a sleevenote that read: "The Desperate Bicycles were formed in March 1977 specifically for the purpose of recording and releasing a single on their own label."

That note inspired Green Gartside to form Scritti Politti and release a debut single on which he itemised the costs of production and manufacturing. He'd formed the band after seeing the Pistols at Leeds Polytechnic, where he was a student. "I saw anything and everything," he told

> "AFTER THAT GIG I WALKED OUT THINKING, 'FUCK ME, TIME TO RETHINK MY LIFE ENTIRELY.'"
>
> **Green Gartside**

me in 2021. "Irish music, jazz, but after that gig I walked out thinking, 'Fuck me, time to rethink my life entirely.'" Indie labels such as Small Wonder and Rough Trade started springing up, the latter eventually forming a distribution network to play the majors at their own game. In 1978, *ZigZag* magazine published a list of 120 labels that had punk acts on their roster; the vast majority from outside London. Although Buzzcocks subsequently signed to United Artists, by which time Devoto had left to form Magazine, and Shelley had taken over as lead singer, they'd started something that couldn't be stopped, while the Pistols, who had inspired all this in the first place, were in danger of being left behind.

McLaren was still thinking in terms of major labels, and talking to CBS, Virgin and A&M, whose Managing Director, Derek Green, was excited by the song "No Future", which McLaren retitled "God Save the Queen". Until now, it had never come together in the studio but suddenly, with "Anarchy" producer Chris Thomas again at the helm, and Bill Price engineering, they recorded the now well-known version. Jamie Reid, whose artwork would become part of the visual identity of twentieth-century Britain, designed a sleeve and a campaign of images such as a ripped Union Jack or the Queen's face with a safety pin through her mouth. Everything was set for "God Save the Queen" to become the Pistols' first release for A&M.

On 9 March 1977, the Pistols signed a two-year deal worth £75,000. This was staged outside Buckingham Palace, for the benefit of the media, a McLaren wheeze that delighted Green. "The Sex Pistols becoming available presented us

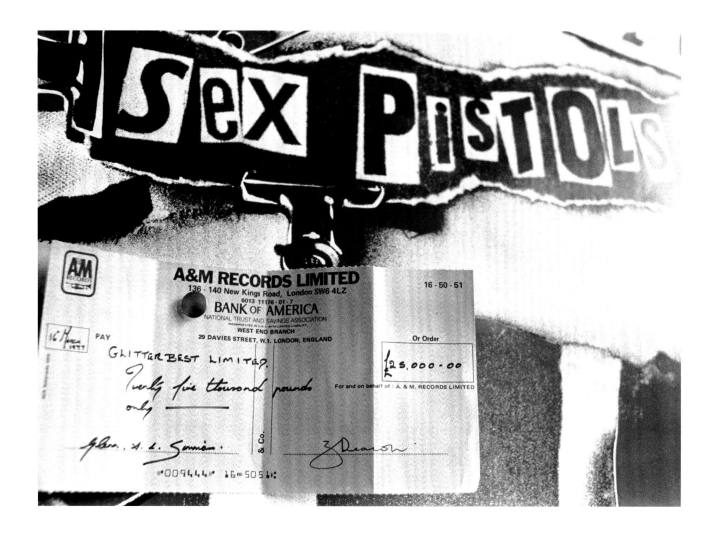

with a unique business opportunity to be linked with a new force in rock music which is spearheaded by this group," he told *Sounds.* "The notoriety which they have already received was not a dissuading factor and would not be to anyone who has been around during the last 15 years of rock music and its fashions. I believe the Sex Pistols will effect major changes in rock music and we at A&M are excited by them, their music and to have entered into a worldwide recording agreement."

However, Green's first shock came at the "official" signing the next day, which incredibly was the first time he actually met the band. Until then, nobody had even told him that Matlock – who'd written the tune of "God Save the Queen" – had left. It was left to McLaren to introduce Vicious with the words, "This is our new bassist. Innee great?!" Things went rapidly downhill from there.

The new signings' next destination was a spectacularly drunken post-signing press conference at the Regent Palace Hotel, before which the Pistols left A&M clutching bottles of their free vodka. Before the press conference, they made a detour to Wessex Studios where Thomas and Price were mixing the single. In a previously

unpublished interview with Tony Bacon, made available on the website *reverb.com* in 2021, Price recalls how the Pistols rocked up in an A&M limo while the kids at the school adjoining the studio were on their break. "As soon as the kids saw this limo, they clung at the fence trying to get over it," he recalls. "They didn't recognise the band, it was just the sight of the limo. The school mistress came out, started screaming at the kids to get back in class. Johnny got out the car and told her, 'Fuck off, you fascist old bastard!' She rang the police. *She* recognised the band! She must have used the word riot, because a Transit [van] full of about 14 police pulled up and bailed out. So I entertained these policemen in number one control room for about half an hour. While the engineer regaled Her Majesty's finest with the minutiae of how a 24-track recording desk works, the band were hidden in a studio around the back … By the time the engineer went back in, they'd all fallen asleep." What must have felt like an attempt at a *Carry On* Pistols movie caper turned more farcical when they clambered back into the car to head for the press conference.

Pages 120–121 – Signing contracts outside Buckingham Palace, 6 January 1977.

Above – Filthy lucre: A cheque for £25,000 on behalf of A&M Records payable to Glitterbest Limited, the publishing and production company founded by Sex Pistols manager Malcolm McLaren, 16 March 1977.

Opposite – The Sex Pistols, London, 10 March 1977.

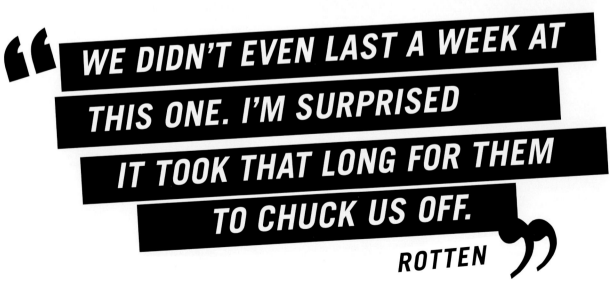

"WE DIDN'T EVEN LAST A WEEK AT THIS ONE. I'M SURPRISED IT TOOK THAT LONG FOR THEM TO CHUCK US OFF.

ROTTEN"

SEX PISTOL IN STORM OVER BRAWL

By Geoff Garvey

ANOTHER storm blew up yesterday over the Sex Pistols punk rock group.

Lead singer Johnny Rotten was said to have been involved in a disco punch-up.

A man was later taken to hospital with cuts to his head, caused by a broken glass.

He was a friend of BBC TV disc jockey Bob Harris, who was also hurt in the brawl.

Solicitors for the two injured men are considering whether to take legal action.

Mr. Harris's manager, Mr. Philip Roberge, said the fight happened in the Speakeasy—a favourite nightspot for pop

Disc jockey Harris: He was punched.

stars in London's Mayfair.

Mr. Harris — host of the BBC-2 pop show The Old Grey Whistle Test—was with recording engineer Mr. George Nicholson, and three other friends.

A tall, blond man is said to have approached Mr. Harris and pestered him to know when the

Sex Pistols' latest record would be played on his TV show.

Mr. Roberge said: "Bob ignored the man who then punched him."

Meanwhile, a scuffle broke out nearby involving among others Johnny Rotten, who was at the club with another group member, Sid Vicious.

Mr. Nicholson was

found minutes later to be covered in blood. He was taken to hospital and had fourteen stitches.

The Sex Pistols became notorious when they used swearwords on Thames TV's Today programme in January.

Their recording contract with EMI was ended soon afterwards.

Their latest record includes the lyrics:
God Save the Queen, a fascist regime
It made you a moron, a potential H-bomb
God Save the Queen. She ain't no human being.
There is no future in England's dream.
But when the record

Singer Rotten: Involved in scuffle.

will come out is a mystery. For A and M Records, the latest company to sign the group, sacked them last week after a wild party at their offices.

PREMIER JIM MUST BEAT THE CLOCK

From Page One.

...rsuading enough of ...em to support him? ...Liberal leader David ...eel said yesterday that ...e votes of his 13-strong ...up would depend on ...Gover...

mandate to push on with full-blooded Socialist government.

It may be even more difficult to win over the group of eight Ulster Unionists, whose most prominent member is Mr. Enoch Powell. This group, which one...

Powell's strong dislike for his former Tory colleagues may not prevent a majority overruling him and deciding to vote for an election.

Of the remaining four Ulstermen, only Mr. Gerry Fitt looks like backing the Government

Scottish Labour men are expected to follow suit.

At Ladbroke's yesterday the odds were 1-2 in favour of the Government surviving on Wednesday and 6-4 against.

RACE ACE VICTIM

TODAY'S WEATHER

CLOUDY, some rain in East, showers, sunny spells in West. Outlook: Similar. London, SE England, E Anglia: Cloudy, bright spells.

SEA CONDITIONS: North Sea, wind mainly N E. force 4, becoming 5-6, seas slight, becoming rough. Channel, N W, 5... Irish Sea:

THE Stomp... for pleadi... counts women Geor... was se Georgia accept report... treated Mitche for deli... on wome platform ing at their rea

46,0 PUPS MORE TH have been crews of el... and Norw... during the Newfoundla Almost seals a pups, accor Canadian F vice.

Golden WINNER of £50,000 Pre... prize M 874658 lives in Numbers for prizes:
8BF 021722
1DK 459763
5DP 592204
3LS 206747
7LB 398395
1MT 090264
5MN 037279
1NS 348249
9PF 009254
2QS 259299
5RF 206868
5BF 539184

VROOM AT T...

Vicious said something to Cook and got a smack in the mouth for his troubles and before they knew it the whole band were at it hammer and tongs in the vehicle. Vicious managed to cut his foot and McLaren was somehow (perhaps not entirely accidentally) walloped in the affray. The hapless posse subsequently arrived at the A&M offices bloodied and drunk, and proceeded to drink as much of the free alcohol as they could. Vicious initially passed out, then somehow managed to break a toilet. Rotten vomited into a plant pot, while Jones was busy trying it on with a female A&M employee in the bathroom

"Total bedlam broke out," Cook later told authors Colegrave and Sullivan, with some understatement, for their book, *Punk*. "The secretaries were terrified. Malcolm was running around. It was just a totally mad day." The chaos didn't even end there. That night, Vicious got into some sort of rumpus with much-loved (and definitely not vicious) BBC DJ "Whispering" Bob Harris, over why the Pistols had never been on his show *The Old Grey Whistle Test*. This excellent TV show showcased aspiring new musical talent, and Harris told them the reason why they'd not been selected was, as he apparently said, "Because I don't like them." Vicious is often said to have then injured Harris's sound engineer George Nicholson with a beer mug, although people close to the

Pistol insist there was no more than a trading of insults. Like so much around the Pistols, there are various versions of the story.

Whatever the truth of it, Green was under pressure from A&M's American HQ. So another splash of tabloid headlines such as "Sex Pistol in trouble over brawl" was the final straw. In a scene reminiscent of their break-up with EMI, on 16 March, A&M issued a statement, declaring: "There is no longer any association between A&M Records and the Sex Pistols. Production of their single, which had been tentatively scheduled for release later this month, has been halted."

Twenty-five thousand unreleased copies of "God Save the Queen" were destroyed, and the handful that weren't – reputedly just nine copies – became highly desirable rarities. (In 2006, one sold for £13,000.) The Pistols' association with their second record label had lasted seven days. "We didn't even last a week at this one," Rotten later reflected. "I'm surprised it took that long for them to chuck us off." As the Pistols' management, McLaren, again kept the money, the *Daily Mirror* grumbled, "Punk group's £75,0000 for nothing."

It was the "*Get pissed. Destroy*" line of "Anarchy in the U.K." brought to chaotic, almost comical real life.

Opposite – The punk band the Sex Pistols, who signed up last week with A & M Records have been fired again, but with a £75,000 pay off. The Sex Pistols with their cheque, and manager Malcolm McLaren at a press conference.

ONE OF THE

ReCoRDS

GreATESt evER made

Out of such carnage, the Pistols pulled off one of their greatest triumphs.

In March 1977, the Sex Pistols were the biggest punk group in the country, but couldn't get a record out. "It's as if the band are a contagious disease. Totally misunderstood," sighed McLaren. While the manager kept trying to find a sympathetic label, the band got back to the day job of playing a gig. McLaren needed somewhere – anywhere – for Vicious to make his debut, but the Greater London Council were putting up all manner of barriers to the band playing live.

US channel NBC were in town to make a programme about punk and wanted to film a concert. Notre Dame Hall – where the Pistols had played before without much controversy – agreed to let the band perform before a limited audience. Flyers for the gig proclaimed: "The fabulous Sex Pistols, introducing new member Sid Vicious." On 21 March, before an audience of just 150, with many more outside, the new member performed in trademark leather jacket and *Vive le rock* T-shirt to a crowd of the Pistols hardcore including Nancy Spungen. It was the first time even some of the inner circle knew they were a couple. Afterwards, NBC filmed McLaren in a black cab talking up the band's significance for an American audience.

Opposite – Johnny Rotten and Steve Jones performing live onstage.

"IT'S REAL, IT'S THEIR EVERYDAY EXPERIENCE OF FIGHTING WITH THE POLICE, OF BEING THROWN OUT OF CAFES OR CLUBS BECAUSE OF THE WAY THEY LOOK.

McLaren

"We are in a country that's economically depressed and out of the large unemployment figures 60% are aged 18," he began. "And when you've got 60% of the unemployed aged 18 out of work or sitting around or hanging around the streets without the music that they feel can capture their imagination and inspire them to go forth you have a whole force that is basically with very little future."

The manager/mouthpiece/boutique owner went on to explain that the punk look and clothing was a total reaction against the packaging of youth clothing in this country, and that writing slogans on their outfits gave youths something of their own. "It's real, it's their everyday experience of fighting with the police, of being thrown out of cafes or clubs because of the way they look; or their parents being out of work and inflicting violence in a pub on a Saturday night because they might be a little drunk." Over a blast of "Problems", the commentator declared: "When it comes to being obnoxious, the Sex Pistols are champions, yet thanks to outrageous headlines their records are among the most popular in England."

"Our music is very honest," said Rotten. "It's the most honest thing that's been happening for the last 15 years." Cook chipped in with, "This

Opposite – Johnny Rotten cleans his fingernails with a pair of scissors backstage at the Paradiso in Amsterdam, 5 January 1977.

Above – Johnny Rotten leaving Marlborough Street Court with Malcolm McLaren after being fined for posessing an illegal drug, 11 March 1977.

movement is working class, from the roots" before a clip of Matlock, obviously filmed before he'd left the band, explaining, "We're doing something no one else is. We're standing up for them and we're standing up for ourselves." Ironically, doing that had brought about his exit, but he wasn't wrong.

Keen to avoid more negative headlines beyond his control, McLaren resorted to his familiar tactic of getting them out of the country. A trip to Jersey ended in debacle, with the band – their reputations now travelling before them – first denied entrance to their hotel and then given 24 hours to leave the island. They headed for Berlin, where Rotten watched East German TV from over the border and was inspired to pen "Holidays in the Sun", about *"a cheap holiday in other people's misery."* It was one of very few songs completed after Matlock left.

On their return, McLaren lined up Vicious's first "proper" gig, a showcase for record companies at the Screen on the Green on 3 April, before 350 people. *Sounds'* Jon Savage praised a fine set and "mesmeric" performance by Rotten, but fretted that the band were becoming a media circus. "There's so much media hype around the Pistols that people will believe anything," he argued, conceding that the band had become potent symbols of "us against them." Almost immediately afterwards, the circus moved up another gear as it became apparent that Vicious was seriously ill with hepatitis. Finally, he admitted his heroin use to McLaren, and the bassist was committed to St Ann's Hospital while his drug problem was hushed up.

Meanwhile, the svengali Malcom McLaren was talking to industry figures about making a Pistols film. Rotten, in another divergence from the manager, didn't want anything to do with it,

preferring to concentrate on music. On 21 April, the band returned to Wessex Studios to continue work on *Never Mind the Bollocks*. One positive outcome of being dropped twice was that the group owned their own tapes and had money to spend on studio time. With Thomas at the helm, they laid down drums, then rhythm guitar, then bass (played by Jones) and overdubs. With Vicious hospitalised for a month and barely competent anyway, Thomas had the brilliant idea of suggesting Jones play his guitar lines – played through a 1972 Fender Twin Reverb amplifier cranked up to the max – on bass as well, but an octave lower. "Bingo!" Thomas told *1977: The Bollocks Diaries.* "That's what people think of as the Pistols sound – Panzer division." Finally, Rotten laid down his vocals in one or two takes, often gesticulating wildly in the vocal booth to get the sounds he wanted.

The band kept sculpting their masterwork. Numerous takes and versions of the songs were recorded. Meanwhile, the search for a record company was still proving fruitless. CBS, Polydor, Decca and Pye had all passed on Britain's most controversial band before an unlikely saviour presented himself in the form of Richard Branson. These days, the now knighted Virgin empire mogul is in the news more for his space missions than music, but back then he was a young, ambitious, persuasive businessman heading up one of Britain's most enterprising labels.

Branson had struck oil with his very first release, *Tubular Bells*, by musically prodigious teenager Mike Oldfield, who'd composed it in his loft and played every instrument on the album. The instrumental offering spent four years in the chart and turned Virgin into the world's biggest

Left – Virgin Records boss and aspiring spaceman Richard Branson

Above – The Screen on the Green, Islington, London, 1977.

GOD Save THE QUEEN

Sex PistOls

independent record company. However, after a glut of proggy rock bands and worthy but poor-selling artists, they needed another big seller. Branson felt that the Pistols might just fit the bill. Despite grumbles in the band's camp about signing with people they called "hippies", the deal (a £15,000 advance, with £50,000 more to follow depending on various conditions) was signed on 13 May in the absence of Sid Vicious, who added his name on being released from hospital days later.

The projected single was still "God Save the Queen", to be released in time for the monarch's Silver Jubilee in June, but band and label were racing against time.

In his review of the Screen on the Green gig, Jon Savage fretted that the Pistols were being "overtaken." With just one hastily deleted release to their name, they were certainly falling behind.

In February, the Damned's first album, *Damned Damned Damned*, had grazed the Top 40, with the Clash's eponymous first – recorded for just £4,000 – reaching No. 12 in April. That same month, the Stranglers – who had a keyboard player and were more new wave than punk, their

songs a distinctive blend of misanthropy and melody – went even better. *Rattus Norvegicus* went Top 5. Then, in May, the Jam became the first British punk(ish) band to appear on *Top of the Pops*, their intense performance of "In the City" propelling the album of the same name into the charts. Also in May, the Clash's "White Riot Tour" took the Jam (who subsequently left the tour because of animosity with the headliners), Buzzcocks, Subway Sect, the Slits and the Prefects around the provinces for 27 dates. The tour was a punk rock landmark that converted thousands to the cause, but the supposed kings of the movement had only managed two small-scale British gigs all year.

Finally, "God Save the Queen" had a release date: 27 May. The hope was that it would enter the Top 10 in the Queen's Jubilee week, thereby hurling an aural bomb amidst the establishment pomp and ceremony. However, there were more problems. Firstly, A&M refused to hand over their metal masters, meaning that the single had to be cut again from the studio tapes. Then – in a rerun of what happened with "Anarchy in the U.K." – workers at the pressing plant refused to

Opposite – "One of the greatest records ever made": the Sex Pistols' "God Save the Queen" single, released in 1977.

Sex Pistols straight in singles chart at Number 11

BBC place TV and radio ban on new single

SEX PISTOLS: "gross bad taste"

THE BBC have banned the Sex Pistols, as their single, 'God Save The Queen', jumped straight in this week's singles chart at Number 11.

The BBC say: "The group will not be appearing on 'Top of the Pops' or radio. Despite the arrival of the Sex Pistols in the charts, the record is in gross bad taste."

Al Clark press officer for the Pistols record company Virgin said: "The BBC's objections revolve principally around the phrase 'fascist regime', If this country isn't one, then one of the first principals of democracy is that the band should be free to sing that line on radio and television.

"The best rock groups in the last 10 years have always been politically and socially outspoken. As it happens the single has gone straight into the chart at Number 11 without the assistance of the BBC, Boots or W. H. Smiths. It shows indications of being next week's Number One."

Rumours that the Sex Pistols would be playing the Rainbow on June 17 have been discounted by a spokesman.

Aerosmith top Reading

TOP US rock band Aerosmith have been confirmed as bill - toppers for Reading Festival on August 28.

The band will be doing European dates with Ted Nugent and Nugent, who appeared at last year's Reading festival, will be making an as yet unconfirmed festival date in the UK in August, but not Reading.

Nugent's new LP 'Catscratch Fever' is released on June 10, and Aerosmith have a new album out in August.

NEWS IN BRIEF

The Little River Band have a three track Max - single out on EMI this week, comprising 'Help Is On Its Way', 'Changed And Different' and 'LA In The Sunshine'.
Rick Hirsch has quit the Wet Willie group to join

handle it, owing to its controversial content. TV advertisements were refused. The BBC and commercial radio stations all banned it, while Boots, Woolworth's and WH Smith – key record retailers of the era – all refused to stock it. "It's their education, isn't it?" Rotten grumbled in *Sex Pistols: The Inside Story.* "They've been repressed. They've been made to feel like they shouldn't have an opinion. When someone comes along with something that fucking blatant, it frightens them."

On the upside, all four music papers – *NME, Sounds, Melody Maker* and *Record Mirror* – made the record Single of the Week. Three of them put the Pistols on the cover, which – in a period when the weekly music press sold hundreds of thousands of copies and were written and read mostly by young people – was invaluable promotion. The single was given another push by a £5000 advertising campaign of Jamie Reid's iconoclastic artwork, which appeared on flyers, posters and London buses despite most other advertisements being banned. In the end, nothing could hold back "God Save the Queen" any longer. Within the first five days of release alone, it sold 150,000 copies.

The song was a masterful and incendiary pop statement. "The pinnacle of the Pistols," as Cook put it in 2021. An instantly unforgettable tune provided the vehicle for Rotten to showcase his razor-sharp talents as wordsmith and provocateur.

★ The time is now right for Iggy

★ Rock becomes like the Hollywood star system

★ Brand new bleached jeans ain't a new look

thing – the word punk to me is a totally irrelevant name for a very important stance of freshness, image plus its rock roots. I like the idea of three or four proud, loud dudes erupting in three chord frenzies and the explorative trip from C to A minor.

Can you imagine what it does to young new wave heads when they find out that there are symphonies in rock 'n' roll too?

To me, it will always be the teenage dream personified. In this stale time for rock and roll maybe we'll get freedom through punk. Let's hope they try and do what I tried in the beginning and get the prices of

Sex Pistols' God Save The Queen.
It won't be on the new album and it may not be out at all for very long.
So get it while you can.
Sex Pistols' God Save The Queen.
Available only as a single from Saturday May 28th at shops with the sign.

Virgin Records VSI81

> ## "THEY'VE BEEN REPRESSED. THEY'VE BEEN MADE TO FEEL LIKE THEY SHOULDN'T HAVE AN OPINION. WHEN SOMEONE COMES ALONG WITH SOMETHING THAT FUCKING BLATANT, IT FRIGHTENS THEM."
>
> *Rotten*

Silver Jubilee

Above – "We love our Queen": Her Majesty the Queen's Silver Jubilee celebrations, 1977.

Opposite – "Stuff the Jubilee": Sex Pistols' boat party on the Thames, Jubilee night. Guests pictured as they are taken away by police.

"*God save the Queen and her fascist regime / When there's no future, how can there be sin? / We're the flowers in the dustbin.*" The lyrics hurled a mind bomb into the vast gulf between the Royal Family and their subjects, the opposing divides of the British class system and the spectrum that runs from entitlement and privilege at one end to generations of wasted talent at the other. The single charted at No. 11 in Silver Jubilee week, a seminal moment in British culture, a perfect juxtaposition of the heart of the establishment and punk rock and a microcosm of a divided, unequal country. Depending on which side of the divide you were on, "God Save the Queen" was either a symbol of everything that was great about

Britain, or everything that was wrong with it.

In 1977, rooted in nostalgia for the British Empire, "for Queen and country" and myths or dreams of a ruling Britannia, the public's fascination with the Royals was even greater than it is today. Millions of households had a Jubilee mug, bonfire beacons burned across the realm, while the day itself was marked by street parties up and down the country. As the televised Royal procession headed from Buckingham Palace to St. Paul's Cathedral, with all the pageantry the establishment could muster, it was as if the economic problems and uncollected rubbish piled in the streets was a mirage. While Britannia revelled in its patriotic fantasies, "God Save the Queen" heralded a "mad parade". Rotten's words blared from teenagers' bedroom windows as he vented about a fascist machine, how tourists are money and how *"Our figurehead is not what she seems."*

On Silver Jubilee day, 7 June, McLaren organised a trademark stunt. The Pistols would perform on a private boat on the Thames (the *Queen Elizabeth*, hired by Virgin for £500), sailing past the Houses of Parliament while playing "God Save the Queen" and "Anarchy in the U.K.". Rotten was unimpressed and it showed. *Melody Maker*'s Allan Jones described the singer's performance as looking as if he was ready for war, or like something out of the horror thriller *Rosemary's Baby*. As with so much around the Pistols at this time, the day descended into chaos.

After the band's set ended, the captain radioed police, who used a megaphone to demand the boat return to shore and then proceeded to clear the craft of its occupants. Several of the group's entourage were arrested, including Vivienne Westwood, Sophie Richmond, Fred Vermorel, Jamie Reid, Rotten's brother, Jimmy Lydon, and McLaren, who shouted a theatrical "You fascist bastards!" at the cops. In all, there were 15 arrests, but the band managed to slip away. In a 2012 *Guardian* interview, Rotten told me that he avoided arrest "because the police stupidly asked me: 'Which one's Johnny Rotten?' I fingered Richard Branson."

Two days later, "God Save the Queen" charted at No. 2, with 200,000 sales in the week, outselling the No. 1 record, Rod Stewart's "The First Cut is the Deepest". Many suspected a plot to keep it from No. 1 and Branson contacted the BPI about an apparent sales discrepancy. Much later, it transpired that the chart compilers had been so horrified by the prospect of a Pistols chart topper that for one week they declared that shops which sold their own label's records could not have those records represented in the chart – so Virgin's sales of "God Save the Queen" were discarded from the statistics.

> ## "ONE OF THE GREATEST RECORDS EVER MADE.
> ### John Peel

Today, Jones regards the sheer effort that was put into preventing a Pistols chart-topper as a "badge of honour," and for many the Pistols were the moral or people's No. 1 – not to mention being No. 1 in the *NME* chart. A triumphant Pistols' camp placed music paper adverts listing everyone that had banned them – from local councils to the BBC – but also thanking DJ John Peel (who'd played "God Save the Queen" before the ban and called it "One of the greatest records ever made"), the music press, their readers and "England's independent record shops."

"If they'd hung us at Traitor's Gate, it would have been applauded by 56 million," Rotten reflects in Julien Temple's 2000 film, *The Filth and the Fury.* "'God Save the Queen' was the alternative National Anthem. But it was never Number One. There was no Number One that week. Whatever we were doing hit a raw nerve."

This was true and the backlash came swiftly and brutally. "Punish the punks," screamed one tabloid headline, effectively declaring open season on the band and anyone associated with them. Reid was attacked by Teddy boys. Temple – who'd already made short films about the Pistols – was punched in Oxford Street. Paul Cook was hit with iron bars at Shepherd's Bush Tube station. Johnny Rotten, producer Thomas and engineer Bill Price were attacked with knives and broken bottles in the Pegasus pub, near Wessex Studios. Rotten's stab wounds led to headlines such as the *Daily Mirror*'s alliterative: "Punk rock Rotten razored."

A week later, at Camden venue Dingwalls, Johnny Rotten was attacked again, and in another incident he ended up barricaded in a restaurant in the West End with his old pal Wobble. It had become dangerous for the Pistols' frontman to go out at all, never mind alone. He hadn't asked to be a target. None of them had. Artistically, culturally and commercially, June 1977 and "God Save the Queen" was a significant and magnificent triumph. However, in some ways it was a poisoned chalice. So much else was getting out of hand, or starting to fall apart.

JIMBO'S CENTRE COURT SHOCKER

See Page 3

INJURED AMIN 'FLEES UGANDA'

By NICHOLAS DAVIES
Foreign Editor

PRESIDENT Idi Amin has fled from Uganda after being wounded in an assassination attempt, it was claimed last night.

Two of his bodyguards were killed when gunmen ambushed Amin's car near Entebbe airport on Saturday, it was reported from neighbouring Kenya.

And last night he was believed to be in hiding receiving medical treatment in a "friendly" African country—possibly Nigeria.

The reports were impossible to confirm last night, as the

GONE TO EARTH: Amin

Ugandan authorities ordered a strict blackout on news of the president.

They refused to accept calls inquiring about Amin, and Uganda Radio—Amin's mouthpiece—ignored reports of the attack.

But Ugandan refugees in Nairobi said the attack was the work of rebels determined to rid the country of a bloody tyrant.

What is certain is that military activity was suddenly stepped up yesterday.

Troops in armoured cars moved in to control key areas of the capital and the provinces, and roadblocks were thrown up around Kampala and Entebbe.

Survived

Amin, 52 next month, has survived at least a dozen attempts on his life since he seized power in a bloodless coup six years ago.

The latest came last year, when three grenades were hurled at him as he left a police passing-out parade.

But the bid failed. Amin survived, although his driver, bodyguard and the would-be assassin all died in the blast.

He has always said he is not afraid to die. He claims he is in direct communication with God, who has told him exactly when he will die — so he knows he is safe until then.

PUNK STAR ROTTEN RAZORED

PUNK rock star Johnny Rotten's face has been slashed in a savage razor attack.

The lead singer of the controversial Sex Pistols group was ambushed by a gang outside a London pub.

Later, 20-year-old Rotten was taken to hospital where stitches were put in his wounds. Two people with him were also injured.

Last night there were fears that the attack was part of a backlash against the Pistols and other punk rock groups.

The Pistols and Rotten, their lead singer, are seen as possible targets because of their anti-royal record, "God Save the Queen." It describes the Queen as a moron.

Ambushed

The attack on Rotten—real name John Lydon—was the second aimed at the group within days.

Last week an art director working with the Sex Pistols was beaten up in a street and left unconscious with a broken nose and a broken leg. His four attackers escaped.

Rotten was ambushed in the car park of the Pegasus pub in Highbury. With him were recording studio manager Bill Price and record producer Chris Thomas.

Bill Price said last night: "We were probably marked down for attack when Johnny Rotten was recognised in the pub.

"The gang cut his face and his arm, but didn't manage to do any serious damage.

"Chris also had his face cut and I got a deep cut in my arm.

"It was obvious Johnny was not

By STUART GREIG

too popular because of the record about the Queen."

A spokesman for Virgin Records, who issued the controversial "Queen" disc, said: "It looks as though punk rockers are in for a hard time.

"The attackers were not teenage thugs but men in their thirties.

"It seems they were aiming for Johnny's face to try to disfigure him. We are worried that this could be the start of a wave of attacks on the group and other punk rockers.

"A lot of people were upset at the record about the Queen, and that could be part of the problem.

"Johnny is a target because he is the king of the punk rockers—the figurehead.

"We're going to have to take special care to protect him."

A Scotland Yard spokesman said last night: "We are investigating this apparently unprovoked attack."

VICTIM: Punk rock star Rotten.

END OF THE WORLD!

But it's all a TV hoax

By JILL PALMER and KENNETH HUGHES

THOUSANDS of viewers were terrified last night by a chilling TV programme which suggested that the world was doomed.

Switchboards of the Daily Mirror and ITV companies throughout the country were jammed with panic calls.

Viewers wanted to be assured that the documentary - style programme's claim about a new ice-age was false.

The programme had reported an escape plan by Americans and Russians, collaborating to set up a colony of scientists on Mars.

But the whole thing was a huge hoax. A joke that misfired.

The only clue that the Anglia TV programme, Alternative 3, was make-believe came right at the end.

The date on which the film was made was flashed on the screen: April 1.

One angry viewer who phoned the Mirror, George Forde, of Peterborough, said:

"The people who put out this programme must be sick in the head.

"Why show an April Fool's joke in the middle of June with no explanation that it was all a hoax?

"I have never seen anything so irresponsible in my life."

Young mother Jane Jones, of Andover, Hants, said: "There are lots of UFO sightings around this part of the country and when I saw this programme I was really frightened."

The director, Christopher Miles, said: "At the end of the film we gave a list of fifteen actors to show it was fiction.

"The message from the film is that people should analyse what they see or hear on TV and radio.

"It demonstrates how we should all keep on our toes."

A spokesman for the watchdog Independent Broadcasting Authority said the programme had been passed by them.

"We thought people were more sophisticated," he said.

NEVER

MIND THE SMALL BALLS, here's ACNE RABBLE

TOO MUCH ....*for one movie!*

color by Deluxe

Russ Meyer's Super VIXENS

R RESTRICTED

...*feast on it!*

WRITTEN, PHOTOGRAPHED, EDITED,
PRODUCED & DIRECTED BY RUSS MEYER.
EXECUTIVE PRODUCER - A. JAMES RYAN

SHARI EUBANK · CHARLES NAPIER · USCHI DIGARD · CHARLES PITTS · HAJI · HENRY ROWLAND
CHRISTY HARTBURG · SHARON KELLY · JOHN LAZAR · STUART LANCASTER · "BIG JACK" PRENAN
DEBORAH MCGUIRE · GLENN DIXON · GARTH PILLSBURY · JOHN LAWRENCE · F. RUFUS OWENS
AN RM FILMS, INTERNATIONAL PRODUCTION

B y July 1977, Rotten was fed up. He was tired of being attacked, physically or in the press, fed up with Sid's heroin use with fellow-user Nancy Spungen, irritated at his bandmates' lack of interest in important meetings and annoyed at McLaren often being unavailable, especially whenever the singer – still on £50 a week – enquired about where the money was all going. Meanwhile, the manager was still chasing his obsession with a Pistols film, which had progressed to a full script with a title, *Who Killed Bambi?* This had been conceived as a *Carry On* romp, with big-breasted women and a love scene featuring Rotten and singer Marianne Faithfull. Marianne's distinctive voice had launched her highly successful career in the Sixties, but at that time she was suffering various temporary setbacks. She was cast as Vicious's mother, who shared a drug dealer with the bassist in real life. Prospective director Russ Meyer was best known for "sexploitation" films such as *Beyond the Valley of the Dolls* and *Supervixens*.

Opposite – Johnny Rotten in reflective mood, c. 1978.

Right – Poster for the sexploitation film *Supervixens*, written and directed by Russ Meyer, 1975.

Rotten instantly disliked both Meyer and the script, although funding issues meant the American eventually returned to Los Angeles, by which time the film's costs had rocketed to a reported million dollars. The frontman was also disillusioned at what his band had inspired – from iron-on "punk rock" T-shirts to the glut of identikit followers in leather jackets. He felt that the Clash were becoming rock stars and was much more taken by the quirkier bands, especially those with female members, such as X-Ray Spex, the Raincoats and the Adverts. McLaren accused Johnny Rotten of "ruining punk" apparently because he demonstrated the breadth of his eclectic music taste on Capital Radio – playing Can, Captain Beefheart, Neil Young and Jamaican reggae acts Culture and Dr Alimantado.

On the upside, "Pretty Vacant", released on July 2, gave the Pistols another smash. *NME*'s Roy Carr compared the Pistols' third single to such milestones as the Rolling Stones' "(I Can't Get No) Satisfaction", the Who's "My Generation" or Martha and the Vandellas' "Dancing in the Street", declaring that it arrived "with the subtlety of an earthquake and trounced the opposition." Like the Clash, Rotten refused to appear on *Top of the Pops*, so a hurriedly made performance video was given to the BBC. For many viewers it was the first time they saw the much-banned band in any kind of action, leading the *Daily Mirror* to froth: "The outrageous Sex Pistols shoot back into Britain's homes … on BBC TV!" The song was played on Radio 1, reached No. 6, and spent eight weeks on the chart.

Opposite – Sid Vicious, Paul Cook, Steve Jones and Johnny Rotten, posed group shot on the set of the "Pretty Vacant" video.

> ## " WHEN WE USED TO PLAY UP NORTH, IT HADN'T REALLY TAKEN OFF ... BUT NOW THERE'S THOUSANDS OF KIDS WHO GET INTO IT AND WANT TO SEE US.
> ### *Cook* "

Above – Sex Pistols in Norway, 1977.

Opposite – Johnny Rotten performing with the Sex Pistols, Copenhagen, 13 July 1977.

Rotten wanted to play live, but suspected that McLaren was actively turning gigs down to retain some sort of mystique. A short Scandinavian tour offered respite from the attacks and gave the quartet the chance to get back to being a band again. With Vicious staying free of heroin while they were there, they were able to do just that – apart from unwelcome attention from biker gangs in Stockholm, where they were given a police escort. They wanted to keep the momentum going in the UK, but the problem was how to bypass all those angry local councils. McLaren had a solution: the Sex Pistols would go on tour, secretly.

Thus, in August 1977 the Sex Pistols started turning up all but unannounced in the regions. Promoters of individual clubs were offered shows on the strict understanding that they kept them quiet, with publicity kept to a minimum as each gig approached. Although they'd played some venues before, they returned as a very different prospect. As Cook told Judy Vermorel in 1977, for *Sex Pistols: The Inside Story*, "When we used to play up north, it hadn't really taken off then. And we just used to get hostile audiences slinging things at us. But now there's thousands of kids who get into it and want to see us, and they haven't seen us at all."

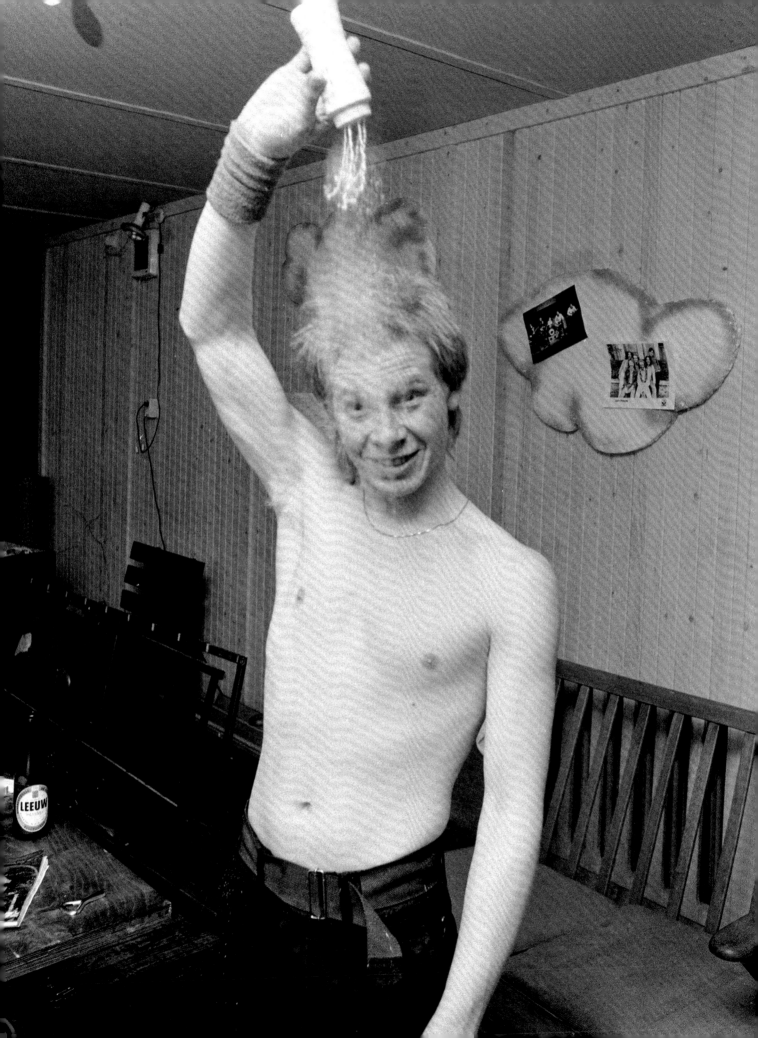

The six-date mini-tour kicked off at Wolverhampton's Club Lafayette, which had hosted other punk luminaries such as Generation X, Bob Geldof's Boomtown Rats, the Vibrators and the Jam. Things got off to an inauspicious start, with fights in the audience. "The first three songs were dreadful," McLaren's PA Sophie Richmond penned in her diary. "Then they were amazing. Everyone pogoed and sang along. John loved it." Some of the time, the band were billed as the S.P.O.T.S (Sex Pistols On Tour Secretly), while other bogus names included the Hamsters and Acne Rabble.

At the Outlook Club in Doncaster, where they'd previously performed in 1976, the Pistols were billed as the Tax Exiles. Footage of that gig has surfaced on YouTube. The sound is poor. The venue is so small you can hear Cook's shouted "1-2-3-4" before opener "Anarchy in the UK" and the security's yells of "Get back! Or there are a lot of people going to get hurt." However, the band sound on top form. In 1977, *Sounds* reviewer Pete Scott hailed it as "a classic." Indeed, away from the upheavals and pressure of the last few months and in venues that belied their status as Britain's leading punk band, anyone lucky enough to catch those summer dates would have witnessed the Vicious-era Pistols at their very best.

Gary Nattrass – who'd bought "Anarchy in the U.K." on EMI and had tickets for the cancelled "Anarchy Tour" gig at Newcastle City Hall – was on holiday with his parents in Scarborough on 25 August when he suddenly spotted the Pistols walking ahead of him in the street. "It was like, 'Bloody hell, they're here.'" He followed them to the Penthouse club and realised they were playing there that night. "We'd heard about the S.P.O.T.S. tour on John Peel but had no idea where they were playing, but once I realised it was happening I found a phone box and called all my mates. Then I queued up from about 4.40. It was a small venue. Tiny stage. I stood right in front of Sid Vicious, who was definitely playing. There wasn't a lot of talk. They just came in and played the songs, but it was great."

Opposite – Powdering my, er, hair: Paul Cook, Eindhoven, 11 December 1977.

Above – Radio presenter John Peel, *c.* 1975.

Vintagerock blogger "Peter" agrees, writing "John was on fire and I was totally blown away. Right place, right time and they captured the mood of the kids. One of the best nights of my life." Down in Cornwall, where major bands rarely ventured, 16-year-old Stephen Corrall was similarly impressed by the gig at the 400-capacity Penzance Winter Gardens on 1 September – where the Pistols were billed as: ? – A Mystery Band of International Repute. "It was a game changer for me," he recalls. "I went in in flares and long hair, but after that gig my trousers got tighter, my hair got shorter and I wore safety pins. I was a pseudo-punk, not a real punk. I didn't get into the whole idea of what it was about. I remember a hail of spit, and thinking 'What is this?' Cos it was so new, but I loved the music." Stephen clearly loves it so much that he plays in tribute band Sex Pistols Swindle, all these years later.

Below – The Sex Pistols, in concert, venue and date unknown.
Opposite – Marc Bolan and vocalist Dave Vanian of the Damned.

The Penzance gig was filmed by Julien Temple, who later told *Punk* authors Colegrave and Sullivan that it was "powerful, proof of just how far they'd come."

In 1977 a great many things were changing, musically and politically. The most commercially significant cultural phenomenon wasn't punk but disco. In July, Donna Summer's Giorgio Moroder-produced electronic odyssey "I Feel Love" spent four weeks at No. 1, laying the foundations for today's electronic dance music. John Travolta's white-suited dancing took the Bee Gees soundtrack to the film *Saturday Night Fever* into millions of homes. The deaths of Elvis Presley and T. Rex's Marc Bolan (on 16 August and 16 September respectively) added to a feeling of shifting ground. "No Beatles, Elvis or Rolling Stones in 1977," sang the Clash, dismissively. Bolan actively championed the new wave that threatened to make his own kind old hat. He was photographed clutching Buzzcocks' *Spiral Scratch* EP and booked Generation X, the Jam, Cuddly Toys, Eddie and the Hot Rods and Radio Stars for his teatime TV show, *Marc*, alongside David Bowie, one of the very few "old guard" stars who met with punk approval.

However, visually identifiable punks were still a relatively minority tribe. This reality is contrary to the revisionist documentaries, which make it sound as if rock's aristocracy were cowering in their mansions. In fact Led Zeppelin's Robert Plant and Jimmy Page even went to see the Damned, and the latter is still a Pistols fan. There were no more than a handful of spiky types in most regional schools, although the records were making significant inroads into the charts and mainstream culture.

Above – Lee "Scratch" Perry, the dub pioneer and "Upsetter".

Opposite – Police officers escort a far-right National Front rally through Lewisham, 1977.

After Shelley took over the departed Devoto's role as frontman, Buzzcocks notched up a run of six Top 40 hits between 1977's "What Do I Get" (No. 37) and 1979's "Harmony in My Head" (No. 32), appearing on *Top of the Pops* many times, initially with 1978's "Love You More". Their most famous song, "Ever Fallen in Love (With Someone You Shouldn't've)", penned in 1977, reached No. 12, was a bigger hit in 1985 for Fine Young Cannibals and has become one of the most widely loved songs of the era. In the long hot summer of 1977, the new wave types regularly scoring hits included Stranglers (who had three Top 10 hits that year), the Adverts, Elvis Costello and Boomtown Rats, while the *Roxy London WC2* live album (featuring Buzzcocks, Wire, Eater, X-Ray Spex et al) went Top 30. The Damned briefly split after a badly

received second album, but while Buzzcocks signed to the major label United Artists, the Top 40 success of their DIY *Spiral Scratch* EP had triggered the creation of the Rough Trade independent distribution network, the bedrock of hits for Joy Division, New Order, Depeche Mode, the Smiths and many more.

Meanwhile, an unlikely union was taking place between punk and reggae. Although the music couldn't have been more different – with punk being fast and guitar-based and Jamaican dub and reggae, notably slow and bass-heavy – the two tribes recognised a shared outsiderly stance which Bob Marley celebrated in "Punky Reggae Party". Black DJ Don Letts played reggae to punks at the Roxy and Culture's "Two Sevens Clash" (meaning 1977) also soundtracked the mood. The Clash recorded Junior Murvin's

"Police and Thieves" on their debut album, recruited Kingston legend Lee "Scratch" Perry to produce punk classic "Complete Control", and recounted reggae all-nighters on the brilliant, reggae-grooved "(White Man) In Hammersmith Palais".

In the autumn, a massive simultaneous eruption in homegrown British reggae, the disaffected black counterpart to the white heat of punk, was cemented when the Stranglers toured the UK with Birmingham reggae outfit Steel Pulse as their support act. Punk and reggae bands also shared stages for Rock Against Racism, which was a movement formed in the wake of a drunken, racist Eric Clapton rant and to help resist the far-right National Front (a fascist political party that reached its peak in 1977).

Some of the most interesting music of the period came when punk started to look beyond three-chord rampages and genres started to cross-pollinate. Siouxsie and the Banshees – who'd been taken on by Polydor after a graffiti campaign urging labels to sign them – were developing a more angular, post-punk sound, while art school types Wire's guitar deconstructions had arguably invented that entire genre. Devoto's Magazine were creating timeless, statuesque keyboard-driven constructions, while the Slits had become a punky-reggae group with a dub producer (Dennis Bovell). So much had been inspired by the Pistols, but was happening without them.

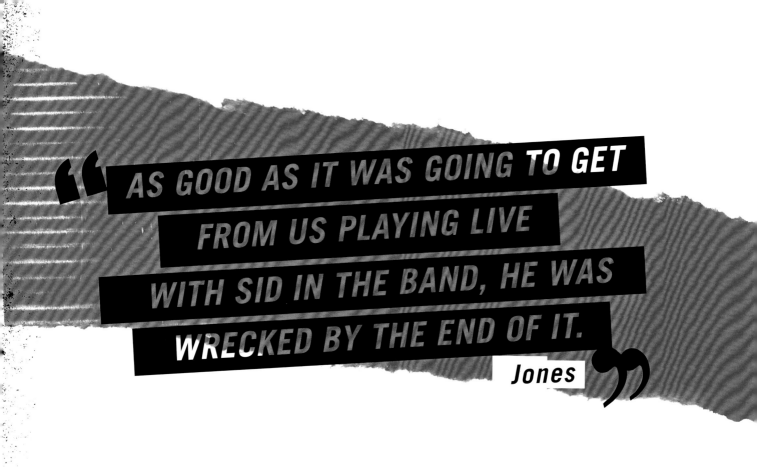

> ## "AS GOOD AS IT WAS GOING TO GET FROM US PLAYING LIVE WITH SID IN THE BAND, HE WAS WRECKED BY THE END OF IT."
> ### Jones

As the band again stopped gigging after the brief triumph of the secret gigs, Vicious sadly drifted back into hard drugs. Jones observed that while the tour had been "as good as it was going to get from us playing live with Sid in the band, he was wrecked by the end of it." Richmond's diary for 24 August 1977 recorded McLaren's chillingly prophetic response when she called to confirm that booking the troubled bassist into an unfurnished Maida Vale flat with a seven-year lease would be OK. "That's fine," he told her. "He'll be dead by then."

Work on the album was dragging on, while the manager was pouring the band's resources into chasing the film dream in Hollywood, with Don Letts' documentary-type *Punk Rock Movie* and Derek Jarman's punk film *Jubilee* beating him to celluloid. With Chris Thomas becoming less available, engineer Bill Price had started producing tracks himself. In June, the Pistols had recorded "Holidays in the Sun", its descending riff resembling the Jam's earlier "In the City". In August, they recorded the second new song of the Vicious era, "Bodies".

Beginning "*She was a girl from Birmingham /*

She just had an abortion," this controversial song was based on the true story of a fan who'd been in a mental institution and followed the band around. "She used to brag about living in a tree," Rotten (now Lydon) told me in a 2018 *Guardian* interview. "She turned up at my place one night with an aborted foetus in a see-through plastic bag. Shock horror and all that, but once you get over it, it's a bloody good subject for a song." The lyricist – further informed by those grim childhood experiences of carrying his mother's five miscarried foetuses from the house in buckets full of blood – respected no sensitivities here either.

The song has been interpreted as anti-abortion, but he argued that it was never that clear-cut. "I could have been aborted. Any of us could. It's about the value of life but also the pointlessness of bringing someone into the world and not caring for them, which is much more savage." The words "fuck" and "fucking" rarely featured in songs in 1977, but the singer said he needed swear words to convey his "sheer rage". "Silly people think swearing is fun," he argued, "but if you use those words carefully they become very clever, full of poignancy."

Opposite – Under lock and key: Sid Vicious at the Electric Ballroom, Camden, London, 1978.

> # "SILLY PEOPLE THINK SWEARING IS FUN, BUT IF YOU USE THOSE WORDS CAREFULLY THEY BECOME VERY CLEVER, FULL OF POIGNANCY."
>
> *Rotten*

Vicious even plays on "Bodies" – his bass is different to the main bass line (played by Jones) and lower in the mix, but he's there. In October, "Holidays in the Sun", with marching jackboots introduction and an excellent B-side, "Satellite", gave the band another hit, reaching No. 8. The song captured Rotten's experiences in Berlin – *"I'm looking over the wall, and they're looking back at me"* – and feelings of claustrophobia and paranoia. By then, after McLaren and Price had compiled several versions from the numerous takes and tracks available, the album was also ready. The title had been changed from the mooted *God Save the Sex Pistols* to *Never Mind the Bollocks, Here's the Sex Pistols*, after a phrase picked up by Jones ("bollocks" being popular slang for "nonsense"). "Submission" was added so late that it initially appeared on a separate, one-sided 7-inch disc included with the album and wasn't listed on the sleeve of early copies. Finally, two years in the writing and recording, *Never Mind the Bollocks, Here's the Sex Pistols* was released on 28 October (11 November in the US). It contained the four singles, "Anarchy in the U.K.", "God Save the Queen", "Pretty Vacant" and "Holidays in the Sun", walls of producer Thomas's "Panzer division" guitar overdubs and came housed in Jamie Reid's now iconic yellow-and-pink artwork. Arguably, the music world was never quite the same again.

Today, Cook and Jones adore it. Lydon, ever the single-minded contrarian, thinks it was too produced. At the time, many reviewers were ecstatic, or thereabouts. *Sounds'* Jon Savage, comparing the album's 125,000 advance sales to the heyday of the Beatles and the Stones, called the Pistols' debut "very powerful," saying it excited him and made him want to dance. "It's a very good rock 'n' roll album … classic rock and roll. Very few albums ever top it as rock as outrage, as the big bad beautiful noise …"

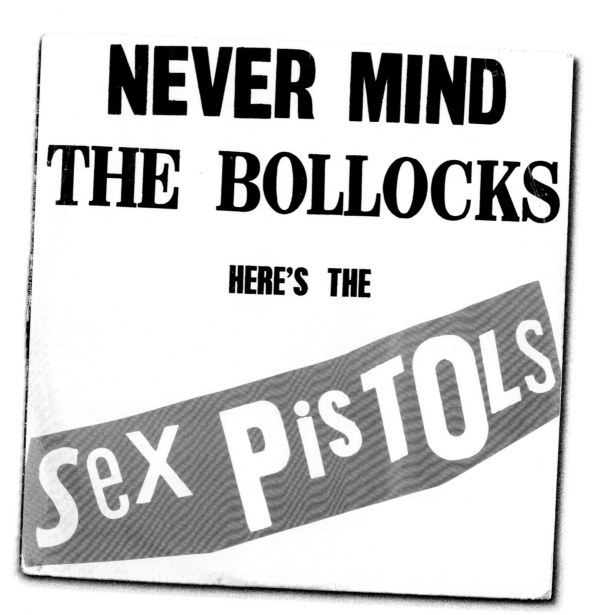

NEVER MIND THE BOLLOCKS, HERE'S THE SEX PISTOLS

TRACK LISTING

Holidays in the Sun
Bodies
No Feelings
Liar
God Save the Queen
Problems

Seventeen
Anarchy in The U.K.
Submission
Pretty Vacant
New York
E.M.I. (Unlimited Edition)

Released 28 October 1977

Label Virgin V2086

Recorded at Wessex Studios, London

Produced by Chris Thomas
and Bill Price

Personnel
Johnny Rotten: vocals
Steve Jones: guitar, bass
Paul Cook: drums
Glen Matlock: bass on "Anarchy in the U.K."
Sid Vicious: second bass (uncredited) on "Bodies" and "God Save the Queen"

Cover Art Jamie Reid

Notes
After Matlock's departure, Steve Jones replicated his own guitar parts on bass, one octave below, creating the album's distinctive "Panzer division" sound. Matlock co-wrote all the songs on the album except "Holidays in the Sun" and "Bodies", co-written by Sid Vicious and the others. *Never Mind the Bollocks* was initially pressed as an 11-track edition, omitting "Submission", which appeared on an accompanying 7-inch disc before being added to the familiar 12-track version of the album. The album was initially produced by Chris Thomas, with Bill Price engineering. However, Price ended up producing some tracks on his own, hence the production credits listing both.

In the US, *Rolling Stone*'s Paul Nelson called it a "masterpiece. Musically, *Never Mind the Bollocks, Here's the Sex Pistols* is just about the most exciting rock & roll record of the Seventies. It's all speed, not nuance – drums like the My Lai massacre, bass throbbing like a diseased heart fifty beats past bursting point, guitars wielded by Jack the Ripper – and the songs all hit like amphetamines or the plague, depending on your point of view. Rotten's jabbing, gabbing vocals won't leave you alone. They either race like crazed, badly wounded soldiers through fields of fire so thick you can't tell the blood from the barrage, or they just stand there in front of you, like amputees in a veterans' hospital, asking where you keep the fresh piles of arms and legs."

Most reviewers struggled to divorce the album from its context: the expletive-filled Bill Grundy interview, the Jubilee, record company controversies and moral panics. However, *Zig Zag*'s Kris Needs argued that the album transcended all this with "some of the most vital rock songs of this decade, brutal, real and full of energy and passion. A stunner."

NME's Julie Burchill pondered the same issues but was more muted, arguing that the album could never live up to the colossal expectations: "What are you waiting for? True love, school to end, Third World/civil war, a leader … The Revolution?" While praising the "great songs," Burchill agreed with McLaren that the *Spunk* bootleg of the Dave Goodman sessions was "a better record."

Despite sales bans at WH Smith, Boots and Woolworth's, the album debuted at No. 1 in the UK, knocking Cliff Richard off the top spot and being certified as gold (selling 500,000 albums) by mid-November. It eventually spent 48 weeks in the Top 75, and has been since certified double platinum (platinum meaning sales of a million albums, double platinum meaning two million) in the UK and platinum in the US, vindication of the sweetest kind for Virgin's investment and belief. Over the years, the album's reputation has only grown. In 1987, *Rolling Stone* named it the second best of the previous 20 years (behind only

the Beatles' *Sgt. Pepper's Lonely Hearts Club Band*) and in 2020 ranked it No. 73 on their list of the 500 greatest albums of all time. It was the third greatest for *NME* writers in 1993. Nirvana's Kurt Cobain named their similarly era-defining *Nevermind* in tribute and in 2013, Noel Gallagher told the BBC: "I made ten albums and in my mind they don't match up to that, and I'm an arrogant bastard. I'd give them all up to have written that, I truly would."

Back in 1977, *Never Mind the Bollocks, Here's the Sex Pistols* received some unexpected coverage when Nottingham Virgin Records store manager Christopher Searle was taken to court for displaying a 9 ft x 6 ft copy of the album sleeve in his shop window, in contravention of the 1889 Indecent Advertisements Act. Although Rotten was the only Pistol who attended proceedings – much to his chagrin – Branson hired barrister John Mortimer QC to mount a defence. Mortimer was also the writer of the popular TV series *Rumpole of the Bailey*, a comedy/drama featuring a charismatic and principled lawyer, "the Bailey" referring to the Old Bailey, London's most famous criminal court.

Gloriously, Mortimer brought in a professor of English studies to argue that the word "bollock" was in fact an Anglo-Saxon term for "small ball" that had been in use for a thousand years, and that a double standard was being applied, because publications using the word (in reviews) were not being deemed indecent. Mortimer won the case. Hilariously, although perhaps not if you wanted the Pistols to remain bêtes noires, the cover and thus the album title was officially pronounced "decent". And Rotten's wonderful public response? "Bollocks!"

Ongoing problems could not be masked by this latest Pistols triumph. McLaren was so wearied by Nancy Spungen's influence on Sid Vicious (and thus the band) that he tried to part her from their orbit "in every single way possible," as he told punk oral history *Please Kill Me*. "Either to get her run over, poisoned, kidnapped or shipped back to New York. She was a bad omen."

Above – Des res: the Pistols enjoy a hotel bathroom on tour in the Netherlands.

Pages 158–159 – Sid Vicious and Nancy Spungen.

The ongoing debacle of the film was still eating time, money and potential new directors. The band was divided into camps: Vicious and Spungen, Cook and Jones, then Rotten, who had become more aware of his power as lyricist, frontman and figurehead. Gigs in Holland passed without major incident, but a rare London show in a 4000-capacity hall at Brunel University proved disastrous. There was violence in the audience, a woefully inadequate sound system and a feeling – certainly from Rotten – that bigger, soulless venues were not what the Pistols were about.

The group ended the year with another short tour, titled *Never Mind the Bans*, of which only five dates actually managed to avoid a cancellation. In Yorkshire, the seminal British punk legends played a club in Keighley called Knickers. When Bankhouse Entertainments promoter Bill Wright was offered another Pistols appearance in the region he thought it was a wind-up. "Everybody wanted them, but you couldn't get them for love or money," he reflected in Leeds-based fanzine *Rouska* five years later. "If you'd offered them ten grand it wouldn't have made a difference. All they

Above – The Sex Pistols in concert in the Netherlands.

Opposite – The Sex Pistols live at De Effenaar, Eindhoven, Netherlands, 9 December 1977.

"NEVER MIND THE BOLLOCKS, HERE'S THE SEX PISTOLS IS JUST ABOUT THE MOST EXCITING ROCK & ROLL RECORD OF THE SEVENTIES. IT'S ALL SPEED, NOT NUANCE ... THE SONGS ALL HIT LIKE AMPHETAMINES.
Rolling Stone

wanted was the right situation and the right club." Which, on Christmas Day 1977, turned out to be two concerts for underprivileged children and families of striking firefighters at Ivanhoe's in Huddersfield (now a Lidl supermarket), for which the Pistols were paid £600.

It was a show unlike anything the Pistols – and probably anyone else – had ever done before. Rotten handed out badges and posters. Teens and young children hit the dancefloor with Vicious to boogie to pop hits such as Baccara's "Yes Sir, I Can Boogie" or "Daddy Cool" by Boney M, before Rotten leapt into a giant Christmas cake and the band and audience smeared each other with food. The implausible event was filmed by Julien Temple, on an old U-matic low-band camera. "But it's right in their face," the director told me in 2013. "It's their full, unbelievable energetic glory, probably the best footage of the Pistols."

As Temple remembers it, the gig at Ivanhoe's was a world away from tabloid hysteria. "To most people they were monsters in the news. But seeing them playing to seven and eight-year-olds was beautiful. They were a radical band, but there was a lot more heart to that group than people know." Another attendee, 16-year-old punk Jez Scott, now a policeman in his fifties, won a skateboard in a pogoing competition and remembers the gig as "very exciting. They played 'Bodies', but omitted the swear words because of the children." Rotten later drily told *1977: The Bollocks Diaries* that kids "instantly understood a song like 'Bodies' because they were closer to the chopping axe of abortion." In 2012, the singer told me that that gig had been one of the highlights of his and Vicious's career. What a shame there weren't more like it. Sadly, the pair would never play together in the UK again.

"EVER GET THE FEELING YOU'VE BEEN CHEATED?"

In late 1977, McLaren put together a short US tour, the stated intention being to avoid the usual rock circuit and perform to "real people". New York and Los Angeles were to be avoided altogether, with a majority of shows in the far less liberal and more intolerant Deep South, where it was no coincidence that they'd be more likely to cause controversy. The tour certainly doesn't seem to have been any sort of attempt to "crack America" – most bands' holy grail – as that takes months of solid touring, not a handful of almost off-the-radar shows. While the Pistols and punk in general had caused media fascination in the States and had alerted the cooler/rebellious kids in the cities, the scene had barely dented an overriding popular culture of the Eagles, Fleetwood Mac, Led Zeppelin and disco.

For all its chart-topping exploits in the UK, in the US *Never Mind the Bollocks* was yet to penetrate the Top 100.

The tour instantly hit the brakes when visa problems (owing to band members' criminal records) led to the cancellation of the first show at Pittsburgh's Leona Theater, and sorting out the difficulties meant the Pistols had to perform on condition of a $1 million bond to guarantee good behaviour. Eventually there were just six dates.

The brief outing finally began on 5 January 1978 (after punishingly long flights from London and then onward from New York) in Atlanta, Georgia. The Pistols packed the 500-capacity Great Southeast Music Hall, located in a shopping plaza on Piedmont Road, attracting the sort of media scrum reminiscent of the "British Invasion" a decade earlier.

Opposite – Sid Vicious and vocalist Johnny Rotten perform at their first North American concert at the Great Southeast Music Hall, Atlanta, Georgia, 5 January 1978.

Below – Sid Vicious and Steve Jones, posed in a hotel room on the ill-fated final tour.

"We're playing these cities because these are the people who will either accept us or hate us," Rotten told the expectant press. "They're not as pretentious as they are in New York." After the gig, *Newsweek* recorded the first words spoken by "anti-Christ" Rotten to an American audience: "Hi I'm John and we're the Sex Pistols." The band were perfectly well behaved and didn't vomit, much to the media's disappointment.

The show itself lasted 45 minutes, opening with "God Save the Queen" (which Rotten introduced as "the new British national anthem") and closing with "Anarchy in the U.K.", which the singer adapted to *"Anarchy for the US of A / It's coming sometime, maybe."*

Here's a report by Tony Paris in Georgia State University magazine *Signal*. It perhaps reflects a young American's giddy excitement at seeing the much talked about Brit phenomenon in the flesh: "The pallid Rotten taunted the audience, whether they were there to abuse him or to hear the band. He was caustic. 'A lot of fun to know we're all going to die, innit? Aren't we the worst thing you've ever seen?' Yet, for all the musical chaos onstage, Rotten was in complete control. He waddled about, looking disheveled and unconcerned, but nothing escaped his watchful eye. They were great."

More seasoned observers were markedly less enthusiastic. "One of the worst gigs they have ever played," declared *Record Mirror*'s Barry Cain.

"It was bad, I mean crapola. Rotten, in tails (minus top hat) left his heart in Finsbury Park. His voice has never been so flat. Steve Jones' guitar is mercilessly out of tune. The timing on nearly every song is hopelessly out."

Ominously, Vicious needed to go to Piedmont Hospital after the gig. He had cut his wrist with a letter opener at a fan's apartment, where he'd been on the hunt for drugs. "It was getting pretty dark around him by that time," Jones writes in *Lonely Boy*, where he also reveals that *High Times* filmed the bassist shooting heroin in a hotel room (the film was quashed by Warners). There were different problems around the Memphis show, held while the city celebrated local boy Elvis Presley's posthumous 43rd birthday. The Pistols' plane was struck by lightning and then the Fire Department reduced the capacity of the Taliesyn Ballroom from 900 to 700, leaving 200 angry ticket holders rioting outside.

At most shows, the Pistols played with armed police flanking the stage, although the Memphis show is generally held to be a cracker, with Rotten in humorously crowd-baiting form. "Is it true you're all into Dolly Parton down here?" he asked to tumultuous cheering. *Sounds'* US reporter Dave Schulps observed: "Rotten leered manically into the mass before him, his eyes like twin knives cutting a path through whatever was in their way, and danced spasmodically ... Sid Vicious, his shirt off to reveal a well-slashed and scarred chest,

Pages 168–169 – Nice little gurners: Johnny Rotten, Sid Vicious, Steve Jones and Paul Cook, posed, group shot, next to the tour bus, on the final tour.

Opposite top – 1978: Johnny Rotten and Steve Jones on the US tour.

Opposite bottom – Sid Vicious and Steve Jones.

> # "THEY STRIKE YOU ON TWO EMOTIONAL LEVELS AND DO IT BETTER ON BOTH THAN ANYONE ELSE.
> ## *Sounds* "

constantly spat on the stage, occasionally jumped up like a kewpie doll in shock treatment … And of course, there was the music. That too was brilliant."

By all accounts, the next show, at Randy's Rodeo, a 2300-capacity punk venue in San Antonio, Texas, was even better. "One of the best rock 'n' roll shows I've ever seen in my life," gushed *NME* photographer Joe Stevens. "Rotten was in top form; the kids were going completely nuts." *Sounds* man Schulps was there again, observing, "They strike you on two emotional levels and do it better on both than anyone else." This time it was Vicious's turn to bait the audience, albeit less stylishly than the singer, shouting, "You cowboys are all a bunch of faggots!" When one of them took umbrage, the bassist tried to assault him with his bass but ended up walloping a publicist from US label Warner Brothers. "Then they [the audience] started throwing things for fun," reported *PUNK*'s John Holmstrom. "Johnny got a pie in the face. After the show, you couldn't see the stage for the beer cans piled on it. I've never seen

such a mess, and the Pistols loved it." So, apparently, did local entrepreneurs. Road manager Rory Johnston later told *Alternative Press* that "People were selling safety pins that weren't real. You could attach them to your ear without sticking them through it."

The next show, at the Kingfish club, Baton Rouge, Louisiana, which followed an overnight bus journey, remains a fan favourite. A bootleg recorded from sound man John "Boogie" Tiberi's mixing desk captures the band in fine form and excellent sound. The 14-song setlist comprised all of *Never Mind the Bollocks* plus "I Wanna Be Me", "Belsen Was a Gas" and a cover of the Stooges' "No Fun". *PUNK*'s John Holmstrom subsequently observed in *Alternative Press* that the high proportion of women in the audience was very unusual in the 1970s, noting "Heavy metal shows were 100 percent male. The club's owner was thrilled to have the band. I was stealing a poster off the wall and he lent a hand. The crowd was drinking and having fun. It was a really strange tour that way."

Opposite – High jinks: Johnny Rotten (with his hands in the air) and bassist Sid Vicious at the Winterland Ballroom in San Francisco, California, 14 January 1978, during the band's last public appearance. Guitarist Steve Jones is on the right.

Above – Johnny Rotten performing live onstage at Randy's Rodeo, San Antonio, Texas, on the final tour.

Above – Paul Cook, Sid Vicious, Steve Jones and Johnny Rotten posed, group shot, onstage at the Longhorn Ballroom, Dallas.

Opposite – Sid Vicious plays bass during a Sex Pistols concert in Dallas, Texas. His nose is bloodied after being punched by a "fan".

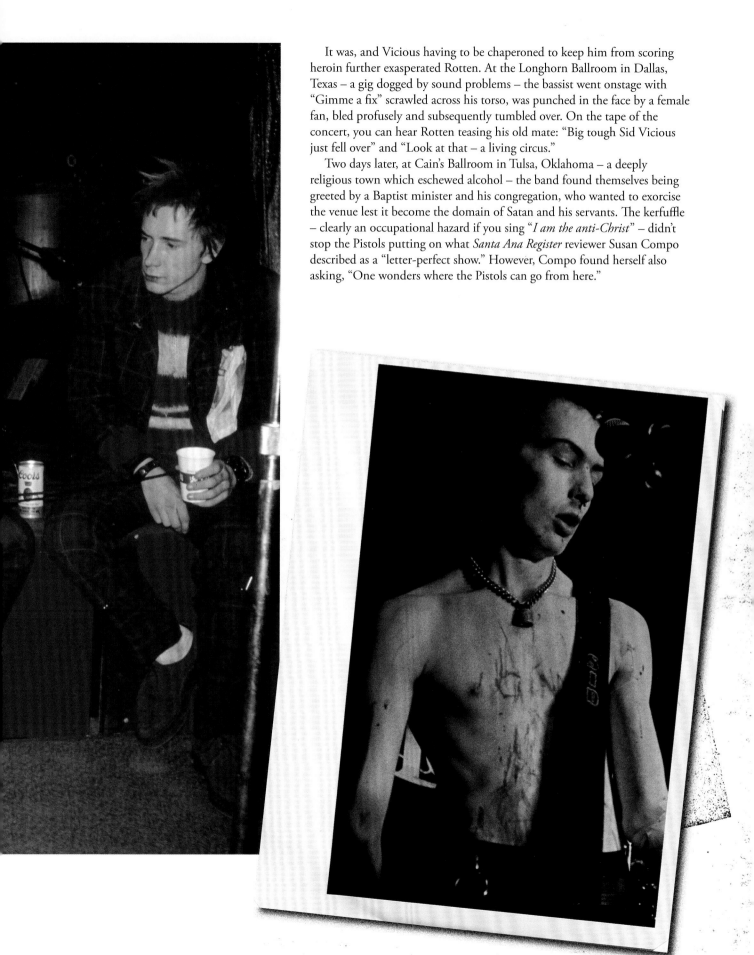

It was, and Vicious having to be chaperoned to keep him from scoring heroin further exasperated Rotten. At the Longhorn Ballroom in Dallas, Texas – a gig dogged by sound problems – the bassist went onstage with "Gimme a fix" scrawled across his torso, was punched in the face by a female fan, bled profusely and subsequently tumbled over. On the tape of the concert, you can hear Rotten teasing his old mate: "Big tough Sid Vicious just fell over" and "Look at that – a living circus."

Two days later, at Cain's Ballroom in Tulsa, Oklahoma – a deeply religious town which eschewed alcohol – the band found themselves being greeted by a Baptist minister and his congregation, who wanted to exorcise the venue lest it become the domain of Satan and his servants. The kerfuffle – clearly an occupational hazard if you sing "*I am the anti-Christ*" – didn't stop the Pistols putting on what *Santa Ana Register* reviewer Susan Compo described as a "letter-perfect show." However, Compo found herself also asking, "One wonders where the Pistols can go from here."

The next immediate stop was San Francisco, for the last night of the tour. After 1000 tickets sold out in 19 minutes, promoter Bill Graham moved the show to the 5400-capacity Winterland, a similar sized hall to the one the band had struggled to cope with at Brunel University. After a Grateful Dead fan complained that the hall would be "defiled" by "punk scum," the promoter recorded that he could have sold 10,000 tickets to a bigger venue had the band not been reluctant to play somewhere so large. By now, people were flying thousands of miles to see what turned out not just to be the biggest show the Sex Pistols had ever played, but also the last.

In the early morning hours before the show, Cook and Jones outraged listeners to KSAN's "Outcasts Hour" with a stream of F-words, and were attacked as they left the station. Later on the same station, Vicious told an interviewer that he'd be dead within two years, and managed to score heroin some time after leaving the building. None of them were looking forward to a scheduled tour of Sweden and none of them were getting on. Even Cook and Jones had fallen out. Rotten was particularly unimpressed by McLaren, not least his plans for them to go to Rio and film

with convicted train robber Ronnie Biggs, who was on the run from British justice. Biggs had been part of the 15-man team who staged the infamous 'Great Train Robbery' of 1963, where £2.6 million was stolen, the bulk of which was never recovered. Ronnie Biggs was arrested and imprisoned, but broke out of jail in 1965 and lived abroad in exile for 36 years. Jones describes the tour as "a complete fucking circus" and suggests that Rotten "thought he was God" by then. All these tensions were starting to collide.

On the night, McLaren sought to whip up the occasion even further by hiring rock critic Richard Meltzer as "master of ceremonies". Meltzer managed to goad the crowd into such near-riotous hysteria that he had to be escorted from the stage for his own safety. The Winterland show itself divided opinion. *Record Mirror*'s Mark Cooper claimed they had "no desire to get their audience off," while *Melody Maker*'s Harvey Kubernik suggested the gig showed that the band had become a "socio-musical statement, a hoopla event. Two parts hype, one part credibility, some really good singles, intriguing flash and an arresting lead singer who makes the network news."

Above – The Sex Pistols perform their last concert, at Winterland on 14 January 1978 in San Francisco, CA.

Opposite – Sid in Dallas.

> ## "WE WERE AWFUL. WE WERE ABSOLUTELY FUCKED.
> Jones"

New York Rocker's Howie Klein decided "It was, predictably, great, including phenomenally exciting performances by the Nuns and the Avengers. The problem was that the greatness of the show was predictable, defeating the whole purpose of the Sex Pistols (who do not view themselves as a merely better version of Kiss or Rod Stewart). 'What a bore,' snarled Rotten backstage." Jones had flu and in *Lonely Boy* admits: "We were awful. We were absolutely fucked."

For *Sounds'* Jonh Ingham, who'd followed them from the beginning, the gig was "ordinary, hardly the stuff of eulogies. John Rotten steadily lost interest, more concerned with looking at the floor than being the antichristuh, the anarchistuh, the vomit squirm. But in its context it was awesome. In that crowd of 5,000 was a mere handful of punks outdone by Grateful Dead T-shirts ten to one. This was a crowd of the curious, and it was exhilarating to watch practically all of them leaping and screaming and waving their arms and doing things they've probably never even thought of doing at a rock concert. That's what freaked out the DJ: everyone liberated from the conventions of cool, throwing not just ice-cubes and cups, but shirts, umbrellas, shoes, anything. At the end of the show he and Sid wandered over the stage oblivious of the audience, picking up stuff until they left the stage

Opposite – Their last concert, at Winterland on 14 January 1978 in San Francisco, CA.

Above – Sid Vicious, Johnny Rotten and Steve Jones perform onstage as security escorts an unruly fan away during their last public appearance, at the Winterland Ballroom in San Francisco, 14 January 1978. Rotten quit the band following the performance.

Above — The Sex Pistols
performing live at Winterland
in San Francisco, CA on
14 January 1978.

Right — Sid Vicious, Paul Cook,
Johnny Rotten and Steve Jones.

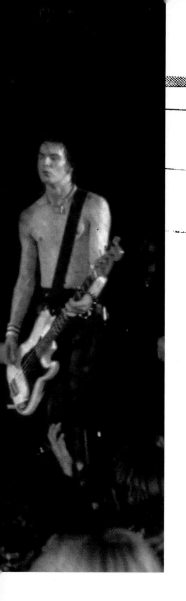

THANKS FOR THE EXCITEMENT, BOYS. YOU'RE THE ONLY BAND THAT HAS EVER MADE ME JUMP, SCREAM, SHOUT, AND TOTALLY LOSE CONTROL. EVERY TIME.

Jonh Ingham, Sounds

with large bundles of clothing and umbrellas under their arms. Sid's razorblade cut on his chest could not be seen too clearly, but the bandage around his elbow was still there. Word had it that he had decided to see how deeply a razor blade would cut. His playing was OK, his actions a hilarious parody of a preening rock-star."

Ingham also observed how, earlier, Vicious had rather surprisingly displayed what the *Sounds* man called "the band's emerging humanism," going on local radio to deliver a speech about injustice, claiming to have written songs about South Africa and God. Perhaps, amidst all the heroin and behind the caricature, Vicious was still what he always had been: a damaged but rather sensitive human being capable of much more. Ingham went on to report how Rotten ended the Winterland performance of "Belsen Was a Gas": "looking totally disgusted. 'Bodies', which followed, no longer sounded ambivalent, it was a scream for life and justice."

Whatever the musical merit or otherwise, the performance saw the frontman's many simmering frustrations finally boil over, and he poured his heart and soul into an emotional and raw performance. After an unexpected encore of "No Fun" culminated with the unimpressed Rotten repeating "This is no fun" while sitting on the floor, the band's cacophony falling apart around him, he uttered the sentence which has been quoted by virtually every punk biographer since and was essentially the Pistols' epitaph: "Ever get the feeling you've been cheated?"

Thus, Ingham concluded his review with a stark "PS": "Thanks for the excitement, boys. You're the only band that has ever made me jump, scream, shout, and totally lose control. Every time." Because, by now, he was able to break the news which would send shockwaves through the British music scene. "John has left the group and the Pistols have split. What's the point of carrying on about how they were praised like gods and – when the equipment didn't fail – played like them, when all that's being written is the epitaph?"

Above – Rotten greets fans backstage after their last concert, at Winterland on 14 January 1978 in San Francisco.
Opposite – Great train robber turned (briefly) Sex Pistols vocalist Ronnie Biggs.

Twenty-two years later, Rotten – now once again using the surname Lydon – told *Melody Maker*'s Neil Mason what caused him to bail out, effectively bringing the curtain down on the Sex Pistols as a meaningful entity. "There was a huge backstage party," he explained. "I wasn't allowed in. Nor was Sid. So that was that. We weren't allowed to stay in the hotel with Malcolm and Steve and Paul. There weren't enough rooms, but of course Malcolm's staff all had rooms, journalists and friends of Malcolm all had rooms. He wouldn't answer the phone, none of his staff would be of any help whatsoever. How can you not know where half of your band is? It would seem impossible wouldn't it?

"The next day, the road crew had disbanded and Sid had vanished. I was left without a plane ticket, without money, without anything. When I rang Warner Brothers, they told me I couldn't possibly be me because they'd been informed I'd gone to Rio." The irony would be hilarious if it wasn't so poignant: the man who sang "I Wanna Be Me" was being told he couldn't possibly be himself.

On 17 January 1978, in the aftermath of Winterland, they went their separate ways. McLaren, Cook and Jones travelled to Los Angeles, then Rio, where they hooked up with train robber Biggs as planned, filming and recording. Vicious – who could hardly have carried on much longer in that state – had overdosed in a shooting gallery after the gig and

McLaren's PA Sophie Richmond took him to hospital in Los Angeles, where he was prescribed the heroin substitute methadone. Later he suffered a valium/methadone induced coma on a plane and ended up being hospitalised in Jamaica, during a snowstorm. There, in a harrowing recorded phone call, he told photographer Roberta Bayley that "I just can't be straight. My basic nature is going to kill me within six months." Rotten, meanwhile, flew to New York – flight and accommodation courtesy of kindly photographer Joe Stevens – where he told the *New York Post*: "I am sick of working with the Sex Pistols." For his part, Jones refutes Lydon's version of events, claiming that for Cook and himself it came down to a choice between Rotten and McLaren: one of them had to go and they chose the singer.

McLaren insisted Rotten had been fired, releasing a statement claiming, "The management is bored with managing a successful rock 'n' roll band. The group is bored with being a successful rock 'n' roll band." By the time Vicious followed Rotten to the Big Apple, the combination of methadone and the altitude of the flight had sent him into a drug induced coma and put him in hospital yet again.

There were no maybes, this was indeed anarchy in the USA. But the Pistols' short, controversial, chaotic but frequently brilliant career was over. For Cook, the end was actually quite welcome. "It was just too intense," he reflected on Radio 5 in 2021. "I don't know if people realise the pressure we were under. It was mayhem. National news everywhere, public enemy number one. Everybody was out to get us and it was a relief when it ended."

"I JUST CAN'T BE STRAIGHT. MY BASIC NATURE IS GOING TO KILL ME WITHIN SIX MONTHS."

Vicious

Paul & Steve

SILLY

THING

INGREDIENTS:
CORN, VEGETABLE OIL,
SALT AND/OR SUGAR,
FOOD COLOURING

SeX PiSTOLS

POP
CORN

From The Film   THE GREAT ROCK 'N' ROLL

AFTERMATH

Whenever something ends – especially prematurely – it's common to look back and ask if things could have turned out differently. This applies equally to whether it's a relationship gone sour or a band that's decided to split. In the Pistols case, perhaps things could have ended in another way, although in all probability they could not. For all the benefits that the various tensions brought to the music, and the chaotic way they operated, ultimately, the same tensions were always going to drive them apart, sooner or later.

At the core of the band was a series of schisms – between Rotten and Matlock, between the singer and McLaren and between Vicious and a long and happy life. Perhaps, had Matlock stayed, there would have been more music than the solitary album and handful of singles produced during the band's short lifetime. However, musically as well as personally, burning briefly as well as brightly was probably built-in. The Pistols were never going to record 27 albums, or shape-shift through the genres. When you've started your career by targeting the Royal Family, the Church and other such institutions at the core of British society, and become the simultaneous most loved and most hated band in the country, where do you go from there? Yes, other songs addressed more open-ended subjects from abortion to youthful disaffection, but in setting their own bar too high, the Pistols became an almost impossible act for themselves to follow. Plus, there's a lot to be said for a cultural short, sharp shock. Like J.D. Salinger, who disappeared from public life after penning *The Catcher in the Rye*, the Sex Pistols said what they needed to, and left the stage, at least in the form we knew them.

THE GREAT ROCK 'N' ROLL SWINDL

WITH MUSIC BY

SEX PISTOLS

WRITTEN & DIRECTED BY
JULIEN TEMPLE

EXECUTIVE PRODUCE
JEREMY THOMAS & DON BO

WITH

Mary Millington

LIZ FRAZER

SPECIAL GUEST APPEARA

THE BLACK ARABS

Irene Har

RELEASED BY VIRGIN FILMS

Sound track album available on Virgin Records V2168, cassette TCV2168.
Read Michael Moorcock's newspaper of the book of the novel of the film
of the record of the group etc. available from Virgin Books.

STARRING

Sid Vicious — JOHNNY ROTTEN — *Paul Cook* — STEVE JONES — Malcolm McLaren — Helen of Troy

At heart, they were propelled and rent asunder by the worsening power struggle between Rotten and McLaren. Perhaps, had they been looked after by a more experienced manager, some of the myriad of problems which befell them would have been avoided. Then again, a more conventional manager might have been in it for the longer term but might not have engineered some of the controversies that saw them make such a splash. Maybe the biggest criticism that could be laid at McLaren's door is not inexperience but that – in chasing the film dream and creating his own mythology, and sparing Vicious a duty of care – he did not always seem to have his charges' best interests at heart.

After they went their separate ways, Rotten challenged the manager – and his companies, Glitterbest and Matrixbest – over missing royalties, which were alleged to be due to the musicians but had been squandered on a film. The case dragged on until 1986, at which point

the Pistols finally got their money – a million pounds – and the control over the group they never had.

Likewise, McLaren got his film. *The Great Rock 'n' Roll Swindle*, released in 1980, is something of a mockumentary-cum-romp. The script is entertaining enough. McLaren rewrites history to star as The Embezzler, the man who created the Sex Pistols, manipulates the members and runs off with the "cash from chaos" taken from various record companies along the way. Vicious is brutally tellingly cast as The Gimmick and train robber Ronnie Biggs joins as Frontman ("No One Is Innocent", featuring Biggs, Cook and Jones and credited to the Sex Pistols, reached No. 7 in June 1978). Rotten called the film "Malcolm's vision of what he believed. Not true in any form." The film and accompanying soundtrack album were both fairly successful, but Julien Temple's vastly superior *The Filth and the Fury* – containing lots of live footage and presented from the band's perspective – gets much closer to what actually happened.

After the initial band's demise, McLaren and Virgin both kept on releasing what they could from the band's labyrinthine archives: the shoddy interview album *Some Product* and ironically titled compilation, *Flogging a Dead Horse*.

Opposite – *The Great Rock 'n' Roll Swindle.*

Top – *The Filth and the Fury*: Paul Cook, Johnny Rotten and Steve Jones of The Sex Pistols in 1977 (film released 2000).

Middle – *The Filth and the Fury*: Nancy Spungen and Sid Vicious.

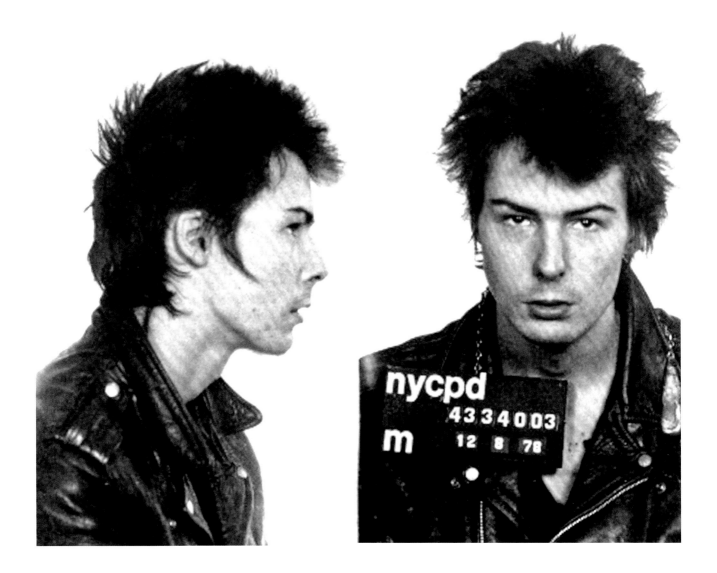

On 12 October 1978, seven months after the band ended, 20-year-old Nancy Spungen was found dead from stab wounds to the stomach in New York's Chelsea Hotel. Vicious – who had been virtually comatose most of the night through taking the drug Tuinal – was charged with murder, incarcerated in New York's Rikers Island jail and later bailed. On 2 February 1979, after his second release from prison, Vicious was found dead of a heroin overdose after a party, the drug that killed him having been supplied by his mother. Rotten has since talked of his guilt for inviting Vicious into the Pistols, commenting "He didn't stand a chance," while Spungen's death was never thoroughly investigated and theories swirl to this day. Friends doubt that Vicious would have deliberately killed Spungen, and suspect a tragic, drug-fuelled accident. We'll never know.

Cook and Jones had some success together as the Professionals. Today, the former is still an active drummer (most recently with Edwin Collins) and the latter has played guitar with everyone from Iggy Pop to Bob Dylan, and has recovered from a spell of heroin addiction to host a popular radio show in Los Angeles.

Matlock formed the Rich Kids, has played with the likes of Iggy Pop and the Damned and is currently pursuing a solo career.

Johnny Rotten, reverting to his former name John Lydon, still records as Public Image Limited, the band he formed in 1978 (initially with Wobble). Their first two albums, *First Issue* (1978) and especially the more avant garde *Metal Box* (1979), are regarded as two of the most seminal examples in the post-punk canon.

He remains a colourful and controversial character, and these days can often be found expressing his fondness for, ironically, the Queen.

The Sex Pistols reformed – with Matlock back on bass – in 1996, 2002 and 2007, playing the back catalogue to audiences that never heard them in the first place. More recently, they were again at loggerheads in court, as Lydon lost a battle to prevent his bandmates allowing use of their music in Danny Boyle's dramatised TV series, *Pistol.* Lydon claimed that this would appear that the band itself has indeed "No Future," although as Matlock observed to me in 2015, "No matter what we've all done individually, nothing is ever going to equate to the Sex Pistols." So never say never.

Opposite top – New York police mugshot of Vicious after he was arrested and charged with assault, accused of attacking singer Patti Smith's brother Todd at a New York dance club in December 1978.

Opposite bottom – Public Image Ltd.

Below – Sex Pistols on the "Filthy Lucre" reunion tour, 1996. L–R Glen Matlock, Johnny Rotten, Paul Cook and Steve Jones.

Their records remain undiminished, their impact registering not just in chart positions, streaming figures and sales but in the continual and continuing reverberations through art, culture, fashion and public life as detailed towards the beginning of the book. They didn't just split the punk atom which paved the way for generations of creativity and culture. They showed a generation – and then successive generations – that there is a different way of doing things, that nobody has to conform to the norm and even poor, working-class, disenchanted or seemingly unemployable youths like them can forge a different future for themselves, as so many have done in their wake. For all the turmoil and chaos at the time, and the various events or controversies since, the Sex Pistols built a legacy they can be very proud of.

> **"NO MATTER WHAT WE'VE ALL DONE INDIVIDUALLY, NOTHING IS <u>EVER</u> GOING TO EQUATE TO THE <u>SEX PISTOLS.</u>"**
> — Matlock

Right – The way they were: Paradiso Club, Amsterdam, 1977.

ACKNOWLEDGEMENTS, SOURCES AND PICTURE CREDITS

Thank you to all my interviewees, recent and more historical. Thank you wherever you are to Mark Chivers, aka Mark Mutilation, the schoolfriend who first alerted me to the Sex Pistols all those years ago. Thank you to the Pistols themselves for inspiration over the subsequent decades and thank you to Emily and Arthur for tolerating my piles of books, interminable writing sessions and punk rock soundtrack – and thank you to my late Mum, for putting up with my punk epiphany (sorry for all those swear words in "Bodies", which I know came as a shock).

SOURCES

Author's interviews (either specifically for this book or originally for *The Guardian*) with Stephen Corrall, Howard Devoto, Green Gartside, Brian James, Glen Matlock, Andrew Logan, Lora Logic, John Lydon, Gary Nattress, Jimmy Pursey, Jez Scott, Poly Styrene, Bernard Sumner, Julien Temple, Toyah Willcox, Jah Wobble.

Magazines and Newspapers *Alternative Press, Classic Rock, Creem, Daily Express, Daily Mail, Daily Mirror, Evening News, The Guardian, Independent on Sunday, Melody Maker, Mojo, New Musical Express, Newsweek, New York Post, New York Rocker, Penarth's Buzz, PUNK, Record Mirror, Rolling Stone, Rouska, San Francisco Call, Santa Ana Register, Sideburns, Signal, Sniffin' Glue, Sounds, Time Out, Uncut, Zigzag.*

TV, Radio and Websites punk77.co.uk, reverb.com, vintagerock.com, Adrian Chiles show, BBC Radio 5, *In Search of Sid* (Radio 4), *Mastertapes* (Radio 4), *So It Goes* (Granada Television), *Today* (Thames Television).

Books Colegrave, Stephen and Sullivan, Chris: *Punk: A Life Apart.* Cassell & Co., 2001; Heylin, Clinton: *Anarchy in the Year Zero.* Route Publishing, 2016; Jones, Steve: *Lonely Boy: Tales from a Sex Pistol.* Cornerstone, 2016; Lydon, John, Zimmerman, Keith and Zimmerman, Kent: *Rotten: No Irish, No Blacks, No Dogs: The Autobiography.* Plexus, 2003; Lydon, John: *Anger is an Energy: My Life Uncensored.* Simon & Schuster, 2015; Matlock, Glen: *I Was a Teenage Sex Pistol.* Rocket 88, 2012; McCain, Gillian and McNeil, Legs: *Please Kill Me: The Oral History of Punk.* Abacus 1997; Salewicz, Chris: *Redemption Song: The Definitive Biography of Joe Strummer.* Harper, 2012 ; Savage, Jon: *England's Dreaming.* Faber & Faber, 2011; Sex Pistols: *The Sex Pistols – 1997: The Bollocks Diaries.* Cassell & Co., 2017; Southall, Brian: *Sex Pistols: 90 Days at EMI.* Omnibus Press, 2017; Vermorel, Fred & Judy: *Sex Pistols: The Inside Story.* Omnibus Press, 2011.

PICTURE CREDITS

Courtesy of Alamy AF archive: 186t; Album: 74; Allstar Picture Library: 30b; Archivio GBB: 109, 38t; BNA Photographic: 100; Dan Moss: 27t; Fine Line Features/Everett Collection: 187t; Goddard Archive: 34t; Kevin Estrada/Media Punch: 178t; M&N: 4, 132, 154, 62t; Mick Sinclair: 138; Moviestore Collection: 17, 187m; Nick Moore: 76; PA Images: 12, 142, 181; Penta Springs: 99, 104; Phil Rees: 187b; Pictorial Press: 19, 29, 67, 80, 88, 131, 140, 191, 186b, 188t; Rajko Simunovic: 133; Records: 184; Retro AdArchives: 81; Some Wonderful Old Things: 134, 135; TCD/Prod.DB: 111b; TheCoverVersion: 155; WS Collection: 144

Courtesy of Getty Allan Tannenbaum: 41; Armando Gallo: 40b; Bill Rowntree/Mirrorpix: 101; Bob Thomas Sports Photography: 8; Brian Rasic: 189; Caroline Greville-Morris/Redferns: 45; Chris Gabrin/Redferns: 51; Chris Morphet/Redferns: 31, 78; Chris Ridley/Radio Times: 147; David Corio/Michael Ochs Archives: 150; David Corio/Redferns: 56; Denis O'Regan: 153; Ebet Roberts/Redferns: 70, 111t; Erica Echenberg/Redferns: 36, 48, 50, 47t, 53b, 58t, 71b, 71t, 77b; Estate of Keith Morris/Redferns: 72; Evening Standard/Hulton Archive: 93, 122, 10t, 30t; Express: 102; Fin Costello/Redferns: 118; Fred Mott/Evening Standard: 38b; Freddie Reed/Mirrorpix: 149; GAB Archive/Redferns: 77t; Gems/Redferns: 63b; George Rose: 170, 177; Gie Knaeps: 161b, 161t; Graham Wood/Evening Standard/Hulton Archive: 82, 84, 90b; Gus Stewart/Redferns: 49, 119, 65b; Hulton-Deutsch Collection/Corbis: 55, 69, 148; Ian Dickson/Redferns: 14, 43, 95, 97, 126, 65t; Jorgen Angel/Redferns: 145; Julian Yewdall: 53t; Kerstin Rodgers/Redferns: 116; Kevin Cummins: 162, 61r, 62b; King Collection/Avalon: 47b; Lex van Rossen/MAI/Redferns: 24, 128; Lisa Haun/Michael Ochs Archives: 61l; Lynn Goldsmith/Corbis/VCG: 169b, 169t; Michael Ochs Archives: 46, 174, 176, 180, 182, 178b, 188b, 40t; Michael Putland: 27b; Mirrorpix: 54, 115, 124, 130, 151; Movie Poster Image Art: 141; P Felix: 33t; Paul Welsh/Redferns: 37; Philip Gould/Corbis: 173; RB/Redferns: 12; Richard E. Aaron/Redferns: 165, 166, 171, 172; Roberta Bayley/Redferns: 35, 83, 175, 34b, 90t; Ruby Ray: 23, 183; Tom Hill/WireImage: 164; Tom Sheehan/Sony Music Archive: 63tr; Virginia Turbett: 6, 143; Watal Asanuma/Shinko Music: 158

Courtesy of Mirrorpix Trinity Mirror: 9, 11, 21, 22, 32, 39, 57, 64, 68, 87, 98, 107, 110, 112, 113, 123, 129, 136, 139, 146, 157, 160, 10b, 137b, 137t, 28b, 28t, 33b, 58b